Organizing and
Managing the
High School
Theatre Program

Organizing and Managing the High School Theatre Program

JAMES R. OPELT

Allyn and Bacon
Boston   London   Toronto   Sydney   Tokyo   Singapore

Library of Congress Cataloging–in–Publication Data

Opelt, James R.
    Organizing and managing the high school theatre
program / James R. Opelt.
        p. cm.
    Includes index.
    ISBN 0–205–12820–3
    1. Theater—Study and teaching (Secondary)
    2. Theater —Production and direction. I. Title.
    PN2075.06 1991
    792'.071'273—dc20   90-20600
                                                                        CIP

Printed in the United States of America
10 9 8 7 6 5 4 3 2 1   95 94 93 92 91

This book is dedicated to my parents,
CHARLES AND EVELYN OPELT.

Without their guidance, support, and encouragement,
it could not have been written.

Contents

Preface

Each year many first-year high school theatre teachers find themselves thrown into a teaching/directing situation for which they may or may not be prepared. The typical teaching duties may consist of several preparations in English, speech, theatre, or various other subjects, along with several extracurricular activities such as directing the school theatre productions and coaching forensics.

In order to be well prepared, the teacher/director needs many resources to organize and manage the theatre program. Resources take years to assemble and compile. At no time in college is the teacher candidate told where to purchase show T-shirts, have tickets printed, order drops, or how to get students to attend rehearsal.

In the following pages I have compiled a resource book for high school speech and theatre teachers/directors based on 15 years' experience of my own teaching and directing high school speech and theatre. Other materials have been selected from several theatre professionals from across the United States. All information has been proven and tested in three high schools in two different states with student enrollments averaging from 450 to 1,200 students. This book will not only give first-year teachers a helping hand but will afford seasoned teachers new and interesting approaches to teaching and directing.

The results from using this text will be stronger high school theatre programs and better prepared high school theatre students. High school theatre feeds our community, college, university, and professional theatres. With stronger high school theatre programs, our students will be well prepared to enter other areas of theatre and, more importantly, life's living stage.

Acknowledgments

The success of this book is due to the contributions and support of many people. The fine people at Allyn and Bacon have shown both professionalism and patience. I thank Mylan Jaixen, Managing Editor; Stephen P. Hull, Editor; and Rebecca J. Dudley and Amy Capute for their help. Thanks also to Lynda Griffiths, TKM Productions, for her help and encouragement in making this text more readable.

Special thanks to: Mr. Stan Adell, camera art; Mr. Barry Alexander, the University of Findlay, friend and text information; Ms. Cindy Asquith, typing, friendship, and encouragement; Ms. Brianna Bender, model; Ms. Melanie Binger, long-time friend, designer, and director; Mr. Ben Booth, model; Mr. Jon Buckman, friend; Clyde Senior High School; Ms. Julie Coblentz, typing and friendship; Mr. Terry Evans, photographer; Gardner Edgerton High School; Mr. Eric Farmer, model; Mr. David Fulton, assistant; Dr. John Gronbeck-Tedesco, the University of Kansas, advisor; Ms. Mary Herbert, designer and long-time friend; Mr. Mark Huffman, Brigham Young University, friend and text information; Ms. Kim Hunt, typing; Ms. Kerry Koenig, model; Dr. William Kuhlke, the University of Kansas, advisor; Ms. Jennifer McDonald, model; Ms. Peggy Muenks, friend and encouragement; Olathe South High School; Ms. Jonna Simon, model; Ms. Janet Smith, friend and director; Mr. Brett Stacks, photographer; Ms. Alfie Thompson, friend and text information; and Mr. Eric Tow, drawings.

I am especially indebted to my family for their encouragement and support.

And finally, thank you to all of the directors and designers with whom I have had the pleasure to work, and to the hundreds of students who worked and performed in the dozens of productions I have directed.

1

Planning a Season

To be successful, a high school theatre program will need, in part, excellent organization and preplanning. Too many high school theatre programs operate from show to show. Directors select shows as the year progresses, rather than examine their overall season and plan accordingly. I have yet to see a program, organized show by show, become truly successful. But most importantly, a poorly planned season is not a good learning experience for the student actors or the production staff.

The four essential steps to follow in planning a season of theatre include setting dates, reading scripts, selecting a script, and deciding on a season and publicity theme.

SETTING DATES

Production dates should be planned a year in advance. In most typical high schools there is seldom a weekend when nothing else is scheduled. As theatre director, you too must fight for clear weekends to present your productions. Once you have established certain weekends for your productions, attempt to keep them the same each year. For instance, my musical was always the second weekend in November, the children's show was the second weekend in January, the spring play was the second weekend in April, and so forth. Your audience and the community will begin to plan around your productions, which will guarantee well-attended performances.

Prescheduled auditions are also advantageous. When students know the dates for auditions and performances, they can plan and select in advance what show(s) they want to audition for. Advance scheduling also helps give your program a sense of professionalism.

READING SCRIPTS

After you have decided on the cast size, reading scripts can be ordered from one of the many script publishing or leasing companies. The main companies for plays are Baker's Plays, Boston; Dramatists Play Service, New York; Samuel French, New York; and Dramatic Publishing Company, Woodstock, Illinois. Companies holding royalty rights to the major Broadway musicals are Music Theatre International, New York; Rodgers & Hammerstein Theatre Library, New York; Samuel French, New York; and Tams-Witmark Music Library, New York. (See Chapter 14 for complete addresses.)

When ordering perusal scripts, also request a royalty and rental quotation. In order for the script company to supply you with a quotation, you will need to supply such information as dates of the production, number of performances, ticket prices, and seating capacity of your auditorium. Many companies will ask what you have paid for royalties in the past. Keeping a show file of your past productions will save you time and enable you to provide this information easily and accurately. Be honest on your contract by listing the correct information. If you change ticket prices or performance dates, notify the leasing company immediately. Also be sure that all publicity releases contain the same information as outlined on the contract. If a leasing company gets hold of a newspaper clipping that states information different from the contract, you will be asked to pay the additional royalty costs.

SELECTING A SCRIPT

When selecting a script, keep in mind the cast size, age range of characters, costume and set requirements, and, if a musical, the dance (see Chapter 6) and voice requirements and what type of accompaniment is needed. Plan a balanced season, one that might include a drama, a comedy or musical comedy, and a children's show. Always offer your students and audience a variety and attempt to appeal to a wide range of interests. Many directors make the mistake of selecting an entire season of comedies, believing that they will appeal to a wider range of audiences. However, it is important to educate your audience as you educate your students. With high school theatre, it is necessary to consider the performance merit as well as the audience appeal. However, always select scripts that will challenge your students and advance their education. (See Chapters 12 and 13 for lists of suggested shows.)

DECIDING ON A SEASON AND PUBLICITY THEME

Once you have selected your shows, look for a common thread that will tie them all together or an interesting idea that will help sell your season of theatre. For example, if the shows all won Tony Awards you might call it ''An Award-Winning Season of Theatre.'' If they all premiered in the same year, you might use the year as a starting point. The fifth year I taught at one school, I presented a show that included alumni performing excerpts from productions presented over a five-year period, so I called the season ''An Anniversary Season of Theatre.'' Other themes I used were ''What a Lineup of Beauties,'' ''An All-Star Season of Theatre,'' and ''We Got Something to Share and We Want to Share It with You.''

Season and Individual Show Fliers

After deciding on your season's theme, print a season flier and include the theme in all of your press releases and theatre programs. The season flier should also include the school's name, the title and a brief description of each show, the dates, and ticket information. Including artwork on the flier will make it more appealing and attractive. Any artwork I used on the season flier was also carried through on the posters and program cover.

Information for the descriptions of the shows can be found in the script catalog where the publishers have summarized the plot of the play. With a little rewriting and additional information you supply, an exciting and informative flier can be developed. I normally printed the season flier in-house, which saved on printing costs.

When mailing the fliers, use the school's nonprofit organization mailing permit, which most schools have for mailing newsletters and other information to district patrons. If your district does not have such a permit, your department may easily secure one from the post office. The mailing cost is a fraction of the cost of a normal letter.

Your mailing list should include those individuals who purchased tickets to past shows. (By keeping the completed order forms from previous performances, your list will grow rapidly.) You could also do a districtwide mailing by securing names and addresses from the phone book or your district board office. In this day of computers, many schools keep a roster of parents' addresses that can be printed on self-stick labels. Address lists can also be bought from the local Chamber of Commerce, or if a community theatre is nearby, they too may have a list that you could use. If money to purchase a list is a problem, perhaps you can exchange a free ad in your program for the list of names.

Often a local business can be persuaded to underwrite the cost of printing and mailing the fliers. Another possibility is to sell patron ads in your programs and use that money to pay for the printing and mailing. I always used money donated by our theatre patrons, then included a note on the flier: "This promotion, including postage, is paid for by our theatre patrons' donations, not tax dollars." The board of education always enjoyed this (see Figures 1.1, 1.2, and 1.3).

In addition to the season flier, a flier should be mailed that announces each individual production. This should include information similar to that of the season flier but focusing on an individual production (see Figures 1.4, 1.5, and 1.6).

The individual show fliers may be a reduced version of the show poster. Most copy machines will reduce originals, which can then be reproduced on regular $8\frac{1}{2} \times 11$-inch paper. Anytime information is mailed to patrons or prospective ticket buyers, a show flier and ticket form should be included. When a show flier is used, a cover letter is not necessary. (For more information on mailings to patrons, see Chapter 11.)

The advantage of a season flier will be improved ticket sales, which will more than compensate your efforts. A little time and money can make your season more professional and get you started on the right foot.

Planning a season will become easier as you build your department. The first year will be the hardest but once you have the groundwork laid, it is easy to make improvements. Much planning can be accomplished before the start of school, so begin your work in the summer. With a planned season, you will have more time to work on each individual show.

SHARE IT! 1987 - 1988 SEASON

NOVEMBER 19, 20 & 21

The South Theatre, Vocal Music, and Orchestra Departments join forces to present Rodgers and Hammerstein's most beloved musical. Winner of the Drama Critics Awarded for Best Musical, CAROUSEL features such songs as "If I Loved You", "June Is Bustin' Out All Over" and "You'll Never Walk Alone". A show for the entire family.

DECEMBER 12

We The People

This is the only high school production in the KC area honoring the 200th Anniversary of the Constitution. This patriotic extravaganza will warm the heart of all Americans, young and old. Do a little flag waving and join us for this special celebration.
Performances at 1:30 and 8:00 p.m.

FEBRUARY 26 & 27

Flowers for Algernon
by David Rogers

The South stage takes on a serious tone in February with the story of Charlie, a mentally retarded man, and the strange interweaving of his life with that of Algernon, a mouse. This is a different kind of play: poignant, romantic, funny and tragic, but with a hope for man's indomitable spirit.

MAY 6 & 7

GEORGE WASHINGTON SLEPT HERE

Laughs will abound in the final Production of the **Share It!** Season in Moss Hart and George S. Kaufman's comedy which chronicles the tribulations of a family man who craves-and-gets- 'a little place in the country to call his own.' You will laugh yourself silly when you join us for the fun of the Fuller family.

TICKET INFORMATION

CAROUSEL tickets are $4.00 for adults
$3.50 for students
All tickets for the following productions are $3.00 :
WE THE PEOPLE...
FLOWERS FOR ALGERNON
GEORGE WASHINGTON SLEPT HERE

Tickets for all performances may be purchased by calling **Olathe South High School** at 913-782-7010 Ext. 32.
ALL SEATS ARE RESERVED

PRODUCTION STAFF
OLATHE SOUTH HIGH SCHOOL

James R. Opelt	Director of Theatre
Jay Roberts	Technical Director
Texanna Ollenberger	Music Director
Greg Ferguson	Orchestra Director
Mary Herbert &	Costumers
Alfie Thompson	
Trudi Kuehn	Hair Stylist
Mark Huffman	Guest Choreographer
	(Brigham Young University)

FIGURE 1.1 Inside of season flier. (Courtesy of Stan Adell)

OLATHE SOUTH HIGH SCHOOL THEATRE
SHARE IT!

Olathe South High School Theatre
1640 E. 151st Street
Olathe, Kansas 66062

BULK RATE
U.S. Postage
PAID
Permit No. 2
Olathe, KS

*A Non-Profit
Organization*

**WE'VE GOT SOMETHING TO SHARE
AND WE WANT TO SHARE IT
WITH YOU!**

FIGURE 1.2   Outside of season flier. (Courtesy of Stan Adell)

GARDNER EDGERTON HIGH SCHOOL
presents
AN ANNIVERSARY SEASON OF THEATRE

GUYS & DOLLS
A MUSICAL FABLE of BROADWAY

Our season opens with the musical comedy **GUYS AND DOLLS** by Frank Loesser and Abe Burrows. This musical fable of Broadway includes such songs as, "I'll Know", "Luck Be A Lady", "A Bushel And A Peck", "Take Back Your Mink", and "Sit Down You're Rockin' The Boat". Tickets will go on sale October 14. Past musicals have been sellouts and GUYS AND DOLLS should be no exception. Dinner will again be served before the Friday and Saturday performances. So get your party together for a delicious dinner and a fun-filled evening of theatre.

A CHRISTMAS SPECTACULAR — December 10
Complete your holiday season by being in the audience for this holiday spectacular. A show for the entire family featuring USD 231 faculty members. Mark your calendar now for this special evening of theatre.

WINNIE-THE-POOH — January 14 and 15
The classic children's story **WINNIE-THE-POOH** by A. A. Milne comes to life on the GEHS stage in January. All the color and fun of Pooh and his friends is sure to delight the students of USD 231. The show is free and open to the public, however, reservations are suggested.

William Inge takes us back to the early 1920's and into the home of the Flood Family in a small Oklahoma town. **DARK AT THE TOP OF THE STAIRS** is a moving, perceptive and effective drama. What Mr. Inge is saying is that there is dark at the top of everyone's stairs but that it can be dissipated by understanding, tolerance, compassion and love. A play that will touch your life.

WILLIAM INGE'S THE DARK AT THE TOP OF THE STAIRS

THE BEST OF GEHS — May 24
Returning alums join current students in celebrating five years of GEHS Theatre. This show happens once every five years so you won't want to miss it. Plan to purchase your tickets early and join in on the fun.

Tickets for all performances may be purchased by calling the high school office at **(913) 884-7101, ext. 210**. All seats are reserved.

James R. Opelt — Director of Theatre

This promotion, including postage, is paid for by our theatre patron's donations, not tax dollars.

FIGURE 1.3   Season flier.

GARDNER EDGERTON HIGH SCHOOL

presents

GUYS & DOLLS

A MUSICAL FABLE of BROADWAY

THE SCORE INCLUDES:

"I'll Know"   "I've Never Been In Love Before"
"A Bushel and a Peck"   "Sit Down You're Rockin' the Boat"
"If I Were a Bell"   "My Time of Day"

November 14, 15 & 16

High School Auditorium

Pre-show dinner served
Friday and Saturday at 6:00 p.m.

Call 884-7101, Ext. 248
for Ticket Reservations

*This promotion, including postage, is paid for by
our theatre patron's donations, not tax dollars.*

FIGURE 1.4   Show flier.

GARDNER EDGERTON HIGH SCHOOL

presents

THE SMASH HIT MUSICAL COMEDY

November 13, 14 & 15
High School Auditorium

Pre-show dinner served
Friday and Saturday at 6:00 p.m.

Call 884-7101, Ext. 248
for Ticket Reservations

FIGURE 1.5   Show flier.

THE PENN VALLEY COMMUNITY
COLLEGE THEATRE DEPARTMENT

PRESENTS

Grease

Friday, April 21
8:00 P.M.

Saturday, April 22
8:00 P.M.

PENN VALLEY LITTLE THEATRE (ST101)
3201 Southwest Trafficway
CALL 932-7600 FOR MORE INFORMATION

General $3.00

Students $2.00

FIGURE 1.6 Show flier.

2

Building an Audience

It has been said that a director has an obligation not only to educate his or her cast and crews but an equal obligation to educate the audience. This is especially true in the high school program. You can direct a flawless production, but if few people are in the audience, your students, administration, and budget will term your hard work a flop. Many directors feel that if parents and grandparents of the cast show up for a play, they have an audience. One director in a high school of about 500 stated that if 20 people attended a performance, she was lucky. I don't see that as being lucky—after eight weeks or more of hard work. High school theatre programs must appeal to the entire school district, community, and beyond.

Building an audience will take as much time as directing a production. For any high school program to survive, a director must also be a businessperson. Once you have built an audience, you must work just as hard to maintain it. Keeping accurate records and complete files will make this job easier. Building an audience can be accomplished through a combination of efforts.

PREPLANNING

Always mail letters to patrons, giving the dates and shows for the current season and requesting their presence. It is never too early to plan and advertise. Even sending season information in the summer can give your audience advanced notice on what is to come. (This subject was discussed in Chapter 1.)

Letters to patrons can be one of the easiest and most economical forms of advertising. A well-written letter can be a powerful sales tool. Most schools have a district or building postage account, so the cost of postage need not come from your Theatre Department budget.

Try to avoid a "form letter" if at all possible. There are many computer programs on the market today that allow you to type a general letter and then input a list of names and addresses. The computer program then prints each letter with a different name and address. You have probably received many of these letters yourself and thought the letter had been personally typed to you. I always individually sign any letter that is mailed to patrons. Sometimes this means hundreds of letters, but patrons often remark that they appreciate the personalization (see Figure 2.1).

RESERVED SEATING

Theatre patrons appreciate it when the high school director takes a professional approach to the total program. Due to small audiences, most schools do not offer reserved seats. Do you know many professional theatres that do not have reserved seating? Reserved seating also indicates that a full house is expected and the production must be worth seeing.

A simple ticket order form (see Chapter 9) should be used to sell your reserved tickets. This provides a record of those who are purchasing tickets. After the production, these names and addresses can be used to keep a running list of potential ticket buyers. After each show, the list is updated and you have begun to build an audience of future ticket buyers. Many computer programs on the market today will easily handle reserved seating as well as store names and addresses of ticket buyers. (The topic of reserved seating is further discussed in Chapters 8, 9, and 10.)

PRESS RELEASES

Press releases for newspapers and local radio and television (cable) stations are easy to write and will gain you free publicity. It is important to have a publicity schedule. A typical schedule might be:

Week 1: Announcement on the selection of the show, which will include the date and a synopsis.

Week 2: Audition results, which could include a picture of the cast looking over the script.

Week 3: Crew results, which could include a picture of crew members building sets.

Week 4: Story about the director and designers or of special interest (e.g., twins in the cast, the drill team performing the dance numbers, the cheerleading squad as cast members, or the star football player in the lead role).

Week 5: Dress rehearsal with pictures of the cast in costume.

Week 6: Ticket update (i.e., how many tickets have been sold and how many tickets remain for sale).

Week 7: Opening night. (This is most effective when printed in the paper on the day of your opening.)

End each press release with ticket information, which includes phone numbers where tickets may be purchased.

If students write the releases, make sure they are proofread. Any information released to the public with misspellings and other errors is a bad reflection on your program.

Avoid offering free tickets in exchange for publicity. Giving away free tickets for any reason can become a never-ending situation. It is hard to justify who gets free tickets and who does not; therefore, it is best not to start.

One of the best sources for information to include in your release is Package Publicity in New York (see Chapter 14) or any theatre books. Figures 2.2, 2.3, 2.4 show examples of typical press releases.

IN-HOUSE PUBLICITY OUTLETS

Look for publications and events within your building and school district where you can receive free advertising. Many districts have district or school newsletters that are published by the administration. These are usually sent out districtwide, which gives your production great coverage.

Most schools have daily announcements that are broadcast to the entire student body. The announcements may even be typed and sent out to each room and read to the class by the teacher. Cast members could take turns doing announcements by starting out the announcement with lines from the play.

Under your direction, students could videotape a short commercial that could be shown before and after school or during lunch. The commercial might include excerpts from scenes, with the cast members doing informative transitions between (see Figure 2.5).

The music department may be willing to include information about your production in their concert programs if you return the favor in your programs. This may also be true for other groups like drill team shows, dance recitals, fashion shows, and art shows.

Write a small announcement and ask for it to be read during half-time or a time out at the football and basketball games. The announcers are usually looking for information that they can use for fill.

All schools have school newspapers that are seeking information to fill their pages. You could even take out a reasonable or free ad in this paper. If your school is lucky enough to have a TV or radio station, this too can be a medium for your advertising.

I always have students complete a form that lists their class schedule along with the junior high or elementary school that they attended. I then send information and a list of names to the teachers of all the students who are participating in the production. Most teachers will usually make mention to the other students and ask for their support of their classmates. Other lists are sent to the various junior highs and elementaries, showing which students from that school are now involved in the high school production. This is most effective if your district has more than one junior high and several elementaries. I also ask the junior highs and all elementaries to add information about our production to their announcements and any publications they might mail out. Having elementary students take home fliers or letters about your production is also very effective. Be sure that you prepare all of the fliers, letters, or announcements so that those you are asking for help need do as little work as possible. They will be more willing to help if it takes only a few minutes of their time.

PERFORMING AT COMMUNITY CLUB MEETINGS

Having students perform excerpts of your show at community club meetings is another way to interest audience members who otherwise would not know about your program. Clubs are happy to have such entertainment and many times will offer your theatre department a donation in return for your presentation. Students should perform in costume when possible. If their appearance at the club meeting is early into your production schedule and costumes are not finished, they could wear show T-shirts.

If you have purchased show buttons (see Chapter 8), distribute them to the club members, leaving an additional reminder of your production and visit to their meeting. Also hand out ticket order forms or have them available to be picked up after the meeting.

One meeting my students always perform for is the local school board. The publicity gained from a 15-minute excerpt at the board meeting is worth a day's work. The students always distribute buttons, and board members have been seen wearing these days after the meeting. Since most board meeting agendas are planned in advance, be sure to ask to be placed on the agenda several weeks prior to your visit. Most board meetings are covered by the local media, so have additional press releases with you to distribute to others in attendance.

Figure 2.6 is an example of a letter that could be sent to area clubs and organizations, telling of the availability of your performance for their club meeting.

STUDENT BODY AS AUDIENCE

Much of the untapped audience is the high school student body, and there are several ways to get students to attend a production.

Ticket Day

About two weeks before your play, sponsor a Ticket Day. On this day students may purchase tickets at a reduced rate, perhaps $.50 less. This should be offered only once per production to avoid losing money. Each student should be allowed to purchase only one ticket. It is better to sell a ticket at a reduced rate than let the seat sit empty. Once you get people to attend your production and see what you are doing, they usually become frequent patrons.

Promotional Week

One way of generating excitement for your production is to organize a promotional week similar to most schools' spirit week or homecoming week. During this time you can offer daily activities before, during, and after school or during the lunch hour. One activity could be a contest, with a ticket to the production as the prize. If you are doing a show with a 1950s theme (like *Bye Bye Birdie* or *Grease*), you might have a 1950s trivia contest. On another day, students could dress in the style of the 50s. On the third day, students could see how many of their classmates can squeeze into a telephone booth or Volkswagon. The ideas are endless and will work for both plays and musicals.

Student Night

One performance of a production can be designated as high school night, with students encouraged to attend with their friends. This should be a performance advertised especially for them although open to the general public.

Student Body Assembly

Performing an excerpt from the show at an assembly can also generate enthusiasm from the audience. (Obviously, never present the entire show; no one is going to pay for what they have already seen free.) An assembly should be well planned. Look for special scenes that can be tied together through transitions and introductions, and of course always end with ticket information. A student body assembly must be a positive performance. This can be accomplished if the director is well organized and the student performers know exactly what they are to perform. Warn your cast that performing for the student body—their peers—is the hardest audience they will ever perform for. It may be best to have an administrator introduce the assembly. This will help set the behavior mood. Students from the cast, perhaps those not in the scenes being performed, should do the transitions. Figure 2.7 is an example of information that should be distributed to your student performers before the student body assembly.

TICKET CONTEST

A ticket contest is also a good way to boost ticket sales. Prizes may be given to the top three salespeople, or you could have a contest between the cast and crews and, in the case of a musical, the orchestra. The winning group could be given a pizza party. If you choose not to have a ticket contest, student performers should be required to sell a set number of tickets. This could be a condition of their contract (see Chapter 4).

Building an audience takes time but each year's work carries over to the next year. As audience members continue to return season after season, your assurance of an audience will make each show less stressful. A bill of one-act plays is one of the hardest audiences to draw. Presenting an evening of one-acts is certainly a great way to involve a large number of students, however, and the large number of actors will in itself draw an audience. But a full-length play or musical will generally appeal to a wider range of audience members. I built my supporters to the point that we could be assured of an audience of over 200 for one-acts! There are many opportunities in any high school to promote theatre. Keep an eye open for those opportunities and use them to the fullest.

Clyde Senior High School

Department of Speech and Theatre

Race Street And Limerick Road
Clyde, Ohio 43410
Telephone 547-9511

JAMES R. OPELT
Instructor and
Director of Theatre

Dear Friends:

Clyde Senior High School will open their 1990-1991 theatre season with the Maxwell Anderson thriller, THE BAD SEED. The play will be presented November 7 and 8 in the Clyde Junior High School auditorium, corner of Vine and Spring Street, with curtain at 8:00 p.m.

You are invited to attend one of our performances of this exciting play about little Rhoda Penmark, the evil queen of the story. On the surface she is sweet, charming, full of old-fashioned graces, loved by her parents, and admired by all her elders. But Rhoda's mother has an uneasy feeling about her. When one of Rhoda's schoolmates is mysteriously drowned at a picnic, Mrs. Penmark is alarmed, for the boy who was drowned was the one who had won the penmanship medal that Rhoda felt she deserved.

Tickets for the show are $4.00, but for a group of 10 or more, tickets are $3.00. We hope you plan to attend one of our performances.

Other Clyde High School Theatre offerings this season are:

IN SEARCH OF THE GOLDEN TEARDROP—December 7

A BAD YEAR FOR TOMATOES—January 17 and 18

BYE BYE BIRDIE—March 26, 27, and 28

THE BEST OF CLYDE HIGH—May 23

Thank you for your time. We hope to see you soon.

James R. Opelt

FIGURE 2.1 Season announcement letter.

Released By:

Theatre Productions
Clyde Senior High School
1015 Race Street
Clyde, Ohio 43410

For Release:

Immediately

Beautiful scenery, lavish costumes, tuneful music, and fast-paced dances describe Clyde Senior High School's production of "Guys and Dolls." The show will be presented in the Clyde Junior High Auditorium, March 24, 25, and 26, with curtain time at 8:00 p.m.

Over 100 students make up the cast, crews, and orchestra of Clyde High School's first musical in 20 years.

Production Director for the show is Mr. James R. Opelt. Musical Director is Mr. Joseph Chidley; Assistant Director, Miss Janet Smith; Orchestra Coordinator, Mr. Ronald Guisinger; Business Manager, Mrs. Tedca Baker; Parent Promotion Chairman, Mr. Daniel Schoenfeld; and Set Construction, Ms. Linda Knudsen.

"Guys and Dolls" is based on a story and characters by Damon Runyon, with music and lyrics by Frank Loesser. The book is by Jo Swerling and Abe Burrows.

"Guys and Dolls" opened on Broadway on November 24, 1950, becoming an immediate success, running for 1200 performances. It has become one of America's most beloved musicals and one of the most widely performed.

The story is about a woman named Miss Sarah Brown, who holds street-corner meetings for her Save-a-Soul Mission in the same vicinity where Nathan Detroit and his cronies hang out. Nathan is the operator of a floating craps game that, at the moment, is homeless.

Miss Adelaide, a singer at the Hot Box, is tired of her long engagement of fourteen years to Nathan and wants him to go legit and marry her.

If Nathan can raise $1000, he can get a place to hold his game. He hits on an idea. Sky Masterson is passing through town on his way to Havana, and Nathan knows Sky will be on almost anything.

Nathan tricks Sky into a bet whereby Nathan says he can name a "doll" that won't go to Havana with Sky. Sky is sure of himself, not only in gambling but particularly with women, and accepts the bet. Nathan names Miss Sarah!

The audience will enjoy finding out the hilarious conclusion, along with enjoying many favorite hit tunes such as "If I Were a Bell" and "A Bushel and a Peck."

Leads for the show are Dianne Schoenfeld, Valerie Orndorf, Jeff Lemmon, and Rick Brock.

All seats are reserved and can be obtained by calling the high school at 547-9511. Adult seats are $4.00 and students $3.00 (18 and under).

# # #

FIGURE 2.2   Press release for musical.

```
Released By:                                              For Release:

Theatre Productions                                       Immediately
Clyde Senior High School
1015 Race Street
Clyde, Ohio 43410


    Clyde Senior High School will open their 1990-91 theatre season with the
Maxwell Anderson thriller, "The Bad Seed." The play will be presented Novem-
ber 7 and 8 in the Clyde Junior High School Auditorium, corner of Vine and
Spring Street, with curtain at 8:00 p.m.
    Little Rhoda Penmark is the evil queen of the story. On the surface she is
sweet, charming, full of old-fashioned graces, loved by her parents, and ad-
mired by all her elders. But Rhoda's mother has an uneasy feeling about her.
When one of Rhoda's schoolmates is mysteriously drowned at a picnic, Mrs.
Penmark is alarmed, for the boy who was drowned was the one who had won the
penmanship medal that Rhoda felt she deserved.
    Forty-eight students make up the cast and crews for this production. Cast
members include Betsy Held as Rhoda Penmark, Steve O'Donnell as Col. Kenneth
Penmark, Tonya Hartshorn as Christine Penmark, Paula Chambers as Monica Breed-
love, Jeff Rader as Emery Wages, Kirk Widman as Leroy, Karen Maines and
Karen Wilson as the Fern Sisters, Jon Eubanks as Reginald Tasker, Laurie War-
wick as Mrs. Daigel, Kevin Hartshorn as Mr. Daigle, and Dean Williams as
Richard Bravo.
    The show is being directed by James R. Opelt, who is being assisted by
Janet Smith. Melanie Binger is coordinating costumes.
    Tickets are now on sale from any cast or crew member or by calling the
high school at 547-9511.
    Other Clyde High School theatre offerings this season are "In Search of
the Golden Teardrop," December 7; "A Bad Year for Tomatoes," January 17 and
18; "Bye Bye Birdie," March 26, 27, and 28; and "The Best of Clyde High," May
23.

                                  # # #
```

FIGURE 2.3   Press release for play.

```
Released By:                                          For Release:

Theatre Productions                                   Immediately
Clyde Senior High School
1015 Race Street
Clyde, Ohio 43410


    James R. Opelt, director of Gardner Edgerton High School's 1990 musical,
"Bye Bye Birdie," describes first-week ticket sales as "excellent." Opelt
said many phone orders were received and that many people visited the high
school office last week to place their ticket orders for the March 26, 27,
and 28 show. Tickets continue to be on sale and may be purchased by call-
ing the high school at 555-1234, ext. 567, or by visiting the high school
office. However, you are encouraged to purchase your tickets as soon as pos-
sible.
    Opelt also released the names of the five elementary students who have
been named to the "Birdie" cast. Sixth-grader David McKay has been selected
to portray the role of Randolph. David will sing in the sarcastic anthem to Ed
Sullivan, "Hymn for a Sunday Evening," and have a solo in the popular num-
ber, "Kids." David is the son of Charles and Nancy McKay of Gardner.
    Other students selected to play the children of Sweet Apple, Ohio, are
Beth Johnston, a sixth-grader and daughter of Dave and Joyce Johnston, Gard-
ner; Gretchen Land, sixth-grader and daughter of Ray and Annalee Coldren,
Gardner; Alisson Ann Pursley, sixth-grader and daughter of Vance and Paula
Pursley, Gardner; and sixth-grader Bob Wolf, son of Harold and Marilyn Wolf,
Gardner. The addition of the elementary students makes a total of 42 cast mem-
bers.

                              # # #
```

FIGURE 2.4   Press release for later in production.

(Darin at table) Good afternoon. (pause) I'm here today as the student director of the spring play, *And Miss Reardon Drinks a Little.*

(slowly moving to coffee table) It seems like we have been spending a lot of time on this set the last few weeks in preparation for Friday and Saturday's performances of *And Miss Reardon Drinks a Little.* (picks up gun) I want to show you a short scene from this weekend's production. I know when you see it you will agree—(pause) this is a show (point gun) you can't afford to miss. (hold)

SCENE 2 pages 19–20.

(Kim at desk) Hi, I'm sophomore Kim Hunt and I play Fleaur Stein in this weekend's production.

In the scene you just saw were seniors Linda Braun, Shelly Richardson, and Nancy Wolf. These three talented women are making their final appearance in a GEHS production this weekend. I have found it both fun and a learning experience working with them and the other cast members, Tye Murphy, Debbie Price, and Greg Shaw.

I am making my acting debut in this play and am proud to be a part of this fine production.

Won't you give us your support by attending one of the performances this Friday or Saturday? Tickets are only $4.00—cheaper than a movie. (pause) I know the entire cast will appreciate your support and you will *not* be disappointed.

Tickets may be purchased from our director, Mr. Opelt, in room 138 or from Shirley in the office. Please be part of our audience this weekend. (pause) Thank you. (to ticket information card)

FIGURE 2.5 *And Miss Reardon Drinks a Little* **video commercial.**

Clyde Senior High School

Department of Speech and Theatre

Race Street And Limerick Road
Clyde, Ohio 43410
Telephone 547-9511

JAMES R. OPELT
Instructor and
Director of Theatre

Dear

Clyde Senior High School will present the musical "South Pacific" March 29, 30, and 31.

To publicize our show, we are offering to area clubs and organizations a program of musical selections and dialogue from our production. We suggest a program of 10 to 20 minutes, but we are willing to work out whatever is most convenient for your group.

This program is offered free of charge. We ask only that you arrange for a piano, which we will need in order to perform.

Since this letter is being sent to all clubs in the Clyde School District, we will schedule programs on a first-come, first-serve basis.

If you would like a program by these talented high school students, please call the high school at 547-9511 and ask for Mr. James Opelt, Director of Theatre.

If you are unable to have our students for a program, we hope you will encourage your club members to attend one of our performances.

Please pass this letter on to the proper person if you are no longer in charge.

Sincerely,

Mr. James R. Opelt
Director of Theatre

JRO/ksf

Thespian Troupe 2494
chartered April 26, 1979

FIGURE 2.6   Performance at club meetings letter.

NIKE JR. HIGH ASSEMBLY

The most important things to remember are to move quickly, move quietly, and act professionally. You are going to NIKE to do a job—do it.

Introduction—Tye Murphy
Opening number into "Follow the Fold"—finish scene
Darin Boysen
"Take Back Your Mink"
Debbie Bialek
Havana Dance only
Julie Gillette
Crap Shooters dance (if time, cue from Mr. Berg, we will skip to "Here they are" through "I've got a little more than dough riding on this one."
Kim Chorny

MAKE SURE YOU HAVE ALL YOUR COSTUMES AND PROPS.

GOOD LUCK

ASSEMBLY PERFORMANCE TRANSITION
Tye Murphy

On November 14, 15, and 16, Gardner Edgerton High School will present the musical comedy, "Guy and Dolls." Today we would like to present a few excerpts from our show. We begin with the opening number. The show takes place in 1940 in New York City.

Darin Boysen

We now take you to the Hot Box nightclub where Miss Adelaide and her Hot Box dancers are about to take the stage in a number called "Take Back Your Mink."

Debbie Bialek

Sky takes Sarah to Havana. They travel from dive to dive and finally, when Sarah has had too much to drink, Sarah and Sky end their trip to Havana with a fight.

Julie Gillette

Nathan finally finds a place for his craps game—in the New York City sewer. We now present the craps shooters' dance, which by the way, was choreographed by Mrs. McAdoo.

Kim Chorny

We have enjoyed performing for you today. Remember—performances are next Thursday, Friday, and Saturday. Student tickets are $3.00 and can be purchased at the high school office. Very few tickets remain for the Friday and Saturday performances, so purchase your ticket as soon as possible. Thank you. See you at the show.

FIGURE 2.7 Assembly performance schedule and transitions.

3

Collaborating Directors and Technical Supervision

For your theatre program to be successful, it must be well organized. A high school program becomes successful when it resembles as closely as possible a professional theatre company. It is important to have one organized chief and several hard-working Indians. Each staff member must know what the other one is doing and what is expected of him or her. Each individual must know where his or her duties begin and end.

It is not enough to verbalize duties—they should be written down, explained, and agreed upon before beginning each production. Those who are under contract should have a copy of their job description attached or written into their contract (see Figure 3.1).

ADULT DIRECTOR/DESIGNER JOB DESCRIPTIONS

Essentially, two groups of staff need job descriptions. The first is the other adult directors/designers. This group will vary from production to production, but could include Music Director, Costume Designers, Set Director, Choreographer, Lighting and Sound Director, and Accompanists.

Many of the duties are the same for each position (e.g., attendance at rehearsals, meetings, and performances; maintaining discipline; helping with lockup; etc.). Some things may seem like common sense, but you can never cover yourself enough. Don't assume anything—put it in writing.

Another important item is for all staff to know that the director always has final say. Again, this must be in writing. It makes your job and the job of others working with you more defined and it stops problems before they begin.

All job descriptions must be adapted to your program; they might even vary from production to production. Figure 3.2 shows examples of six different job descriptions for adult directors/designers.

STUDENT JOB DESCRIPTIONS

The second set of job descriptions outline the duties for students who hold key positions during production.

Remember: The production you direct is not *your* show—it is the *students'* show. Therefore, the more the students are involved, the better. Responsible students in key positions will reduce the director's workload. However, everyone needs guidance and direction. Many programs fail because directors have given students responsibility without supervision. Know what your students are doing and let them know what is expected of them.

Again, many items will be the same for each position. Everyone must read the script, help organize equipment, and keep other students informed about rehearsal times and performances.

Most high school students are involved in many different activities. Keeping them informed can become a job in itself. But when students remind students and encourage their dedication and cooperation, the results are overwhelming. I have always had 98–100 percent attendance at rehearsals and work sessions. I know this is due in part to organized student leaders.

Job descriptions for students will vary from production to production. These can include Makeup, Lights and Sound, and Props and Stage Crews (see Figure 3.3).

Position: _____

It is hereby agreed by and between Unified School District No. 231, Johnson County, State of Kansas, represented by _____ and _____

       Herein after called the "Employee":

That the employee agrees to carry out the following duties which are over and above any duties that may be included in any other existing contracts with the aforementioned school.

The music director will attend all music rehearsals, dress rehearsals, and performances. His work will include both choral and individual singing. It is understood that strict discipline will be maintained at all times during rehearsals. The music director will report directly to Jim Opelt, production director, who will have final say in all matters. Production dates for the musical are November 11, 12, and 13, 1991.

That said employee will be paid according to the following scale:

                          Flat rate for entire job $ _____

_____   _____
        Date   Signature of Employer

_____   _____
        Date   Signature of Principal

_____   _____
        Date   Approval of Superintendent

FIGURE 3.1   Musical director contract.

MUSIC DIRECTOR FOR MUSICAL

1. Will attend all music rehearsals, dress rehearsals, and performances.
2. Will work with both large group and individuals.
3. Will maintain strict discipline at each rehearsal.
4. Will arrange for accompanists for each rehearsal, performance, and special assemblies.
5. Will prepare materials for all music rehearsals.
6. Will see that all music books are cleaned for return to library.
7. Will prepare an agenda and have it approved by Mr. Opelt before each scheduled music rehearsal. Will have the agenda posted on the callboard prior to each rehearsal.
8. Will help supervise at dress rehearsals and performances and help with cleanup and lockup.
9. Will arrange for pianos, and their tuning if needed, for rehearsals, performances, and special assemblies.
10. Will have rehearsal tapes made for choreographer and work with same on any music problems that deal with dancing.
11. Will attend all production staff meetings called by Mr. Opelt.
12. Will report directly to Mr. Opelt, production director, who will have final say in all matters.
13. Will assist with auditions and casting of the show.

COSTUME DESIGNER/SUPERVISOR FOR MUSICAL

1. Will attend all costume work sessions, dress rehearsals, and performances.
2. Will purchase all needed materials and supplies for costumes after being approved by Mr. Opelt.
3. Will supervise costume crew.
4. Will maintain strict discipline at each work session.
5. Will prepare an agenda and have it approved by Mr. Opelt before each work session. Will have the agenda posted on the callboard prior to each work session.
6. Will contact parents when costume materials are sent home for construction.
7. Will organize parents to help with costumes.
8. Will see that all borrowed costumes are returned.
9. Will keep accurate records of all costumes loaned to students and see that all are returned.
10. Will supervise cleanup of dressing rooms during strike.
11. Will help supervise at dress rehearsals and performances and help with cleanup and lockup.

FIGURE 3.2   Job descriptions.

12. Will attend all production staff meetings called by Mr. Opelt.
13. Will report directly to Mr. Opelt, production director, who will have final say in all matters.

SET DESIGNER FOR MUSICAL

1. Will schedule work sessions for construction crew.
2. Will supervise construction crew, stage crew, and prop crew during work sessions, dress rehearsals, performances, and special assemblies.
3. Will maintain strict discipline at all times.
4. Will encourage good safety habits while working on stage.
5. Will supervise cleanup of the stage area after all work sessions, performances, and rehearsals.
6. Will help with lockup.
7. Will select stage crew from construction crew based on attendance and work habits.
8. Will supervise strike and return all borrowed or rental equipment.
9. Will order needed materials after receiving approval from Mr. Opelt.
10. Will attend all production meetings called by Mr. Opelt.
11. Will report directly to Mr. Opelt, production director, who will have final say in all matters.

CHOREOGRAPHER FOR MUSICAL

1. Will attend all dance rehearsals, dress rehearsals, and performances.
2. Will work with large group and individual dancing.
3. Will maintain strict discipline at each rehearsal.
4. Will work with music director on any problems that deal with dancing.
5. Will prepare an agenda and have it approved by Mr. Opelt before each scheduled dance rehearsal. Will have the agenda posted on the callboard prior to each rehearsal.
6. Will help supervise at dress rehearsals and performances and help with cleanup and lockup.
7. Will attend all production staff meetings called by Mr. Opelt.
8. Will report directly to Mr. Opelt, production director, who will have final say in all matters.

LIGHTING AND SOUND DESIGNER FOR MUSCIAL

1. Will schedule work sessions for lighting and sound crew.
2. Will supervise lighting and sound crew during all work sessions, dress rehearsals, performances, and special assemblies. *(continued)*

FIGURE 3.2 Continued.

3. Will maintain strict discipline at all times.
4. Will encourage good safety habits while working on stage.
5. Will supervise cleanup on the stage area and light booth after all work sessions, rehearsals, and performances.
6. Will help with lockup.
7. Will supervise strike and return all borrowed or rental equipment used by the lighting and sound crew.
8. Will order needed materials after receiving approval from Mr. Opelt.
9. Will attend all production meetings, work sessions, dress rehearsals, and performances.
10. Will report directly to Mr. Opelt, production director, who will have final say in all matters.

ACCOMPANIST FOR MUSICAL

1. Will attend all music rehearsals, dress rehearsals, performances, and scheduled special assemblies.
2. Will have music prepared for each rehearsal.
3. Will work with both large group and individuals.
4. Will record tapes for choreographer and others when needed.
5. Will accompany auditions.
6. Will help music director run music rehearsals, with music director being in charge.
7. Will report directly to Mr. Opelt, production director, who will have final say in all matters.

FIGURE 3.2   Continued.

MAKEUP CREW

1. Read script.
2. Inventory makeup and report to Mr. Opelt any makeup that needs to be purchased.
3. Organize and distribute makeup call.
4. Distribute call reminders or write announcement.
5. Prepare makeup room for rehearsals and performances (15 minutes before first call).
6. Clean makeup room after each rehearsal and performance.
7. Secure supplies after each rehearsal and performance.
8. Secure supplies after final performance.

LIGHTS AND SOUND CREW

1. Read script.
2. Make sound effects tape.
3. Call meeting.
4. Help set lights.
5. Check out headsets before each rehearsal and performance.
6. Test headsets before each rehearsal and performance.
7. Check in headsets and store them after each rehearsal and performance.
8. Test lights and sound one hour before each performance.
9. Send out rehearsal reminders.

PROPS AND STAGE CREW

1. Read script.
2. Call crew meeting (Stage Manager/Crew Heads).
3. Organize prop list.
4. Locate all props.
5. Keep inventory of all props.
6. Organize all props and scenery on stage.
7. Distribute rehearsal reminders.
8. Vacuum stage before each rehearsal and performance.
9. Set stage 15 minutes before each rehearsal and one hour before each performance.
10. Secure all props and set pieces after each rehearsal and performance.
11. Inventory all props after each rehearsal or performance.
12. Check out crew T-shirts within one week of the last performance (Stage Manager/Crew Heads).
14. Return all props within one week of the last performance.

FIGURE 3.3   Job descriptions.

4

Auditions and Rehearsing the Play

The primary concern of most high school theatre directors around the country seems to be student attendance at rehearsals. Especially in smaller schools, only the very few dedicated theatre students seem to make play rehearsal a priority.

Most high school students want to do the least amount of work for the greatest reward. Many students also want to be a part of as many activities as possible and consequently end up doing none of them justice. The demands on their time can be overwhelming. Also, as high school students become increasingly more involved in the work force, extracurricular theatre activities become less important or sometimes impossible to attend.

Directors have told me they are lucky if they have 50 percent of their cast at rehearsals, and many directors are unable to assemble the entire cast until the final dress rehearsal. One rehearsal with the entire cast! However, if such is the case, the director is at fault. First and foremost, students must be taught the importance of rehearsals. This is done by example. You, as the director, must look at rehearsals as being important and not just another after-school duty assignment. Let students know by your actions and words that directing is as important to you as your classroom work. This will then influence the students.

REHEARSAL SCHEDULES

Always begin and end rehearsals on time. This not only shows that you are organized but it sets a schedule that the students can plan around. If students know exactly when rehearsals are going to be held, it helps them organize their time.

It is important to have a copy of the rehearsal schedule available during auditions. Obviously, it is better for a student to back out of auditioning because of schedule and time conflicts than to quit the show two or three weeks into rehearsals. Rehearsal schedules can take many shapes; however, try to include as much information about each individual rehearsal as possible.

Several sample rehearsal schedules are shown in Figures 4.1 through 4.4.

AUDITION INFORMATION SHEET

Along with the schedule of rehearsals, auditioning students need to be aware of attendance policies and the commitments associated with being a member of the cast. This information is listed on an audition information sheet, which might also include a list of the directors, an explanation of the callboard, a word about maintaining good grades, costume information, the audition procedure, and a final word of encouragement. This allows the students to know exactly what type of commitment they are making toward the production. A copy of the information sheet should also be given to those individuals who request a crew appointment and, when presenting a musical, to the orchestra members (see Figure 4.5 and 4.6).

Audition procedures will vary from director to director. I always hold "closed" auditions. In a closed audition, only the student who is auditioning and the director(s) is in the room. By having a closed audition, the director is not leaving himself or herself open to criticism about the reasons why one student was cast and another was not. In a closed audition, no one but the director knows how each student auditioned.

For a play, I have students read cold from the script, usually in male and female pairs. If more information is needed, I have them improvise a character or scene. For a musical, students prepare a dance, gymnastics routine, or organized movement to music of their choice; sing a prepared selection, also of their choice; and read cold from the script.

Because high school students are normally less experienced in dance, students can choose to dance in pairs.

High school theatre directors may sometimes need to deal with big student egos. Many times students who do not receive the part they want or perhaps receive a part they feel is "too small" will quit the show even before rehearsals begin. My rule for students quitting a show after being cast is that he or she cannot audition for another show during the school year or season in which he or she quit. The only exceptions are for physical problems that would not allow the student to continue his or her role. I always made sure the administration was in agreement with this rule, and in 14 years of teaching it was never challenged. Such a rule teaches students responsibility and commitment. It also gives you, as director, peace-of-mind that you will not have to recast a character in the middle of rehearsals.

AUDITION FORMS

When making an audition form, always include a section that asks the student to list the times he or she is *not* available for rehearsal. This is the first section I look at when casting. If there is a student who has schedule conflicts but is the only one to fill a particular part, then I suggest you talk with him or her before posting the cast and explain the commitment. I have even included parents in such a meeting, which helps to confirm the commitment and responsibility to the production. Also include a place on the form that asks the student if he or she has a job. Most students will find it hard to schedule around both a job and play rehearsal. The director should not have to work around any student's schedule, and with a cast of 40 to 50 it is impossible. Many times when students realize that you are concerned about them and their schedules, they become twice as dedicated to the production.

To ensure that everyone understands the commitment, include a section on the audition form for both the auditioning student and his or her parent to sign. A possible statement might be: "Have you read and agreed to the commitments as listed on the information form?" For the parents: "I understand the commitments associated with the position for which the above named student is applying and furthermore agree to support him/her if he/she is chosen for this activity."

Also, do not forget the crew members—they are as important as the cast. The same procedures should be followed when selecting crews.

Figures 4.7 and 4.8 show a sample (front and back) crew application form.

STUDENT INFORMATION FORM

After auditions have been completed, have the students fill out a Student Information Form. This will be useful throughout the rehearsal period and production. The form should include a place for the current mailing address of each student's parents. You will need this address when mailing the Attendance Letter (see next section), ticket information, changes of rehearsals, and so on.

A place for the student's schedule should also be provided on the form. This will save you a great deal of time when you need to contact the cast or an individual student concerning the production (see Figure 4.9).

ATTENDANCE LETTER

An Attendance Letter sent to parents and signed by the director and administrators is very helpful at the beginning of the rehearsal period. This will emphasize the importance of rehearsals and restate the attendance policy. It also helps the parents understand what is expected of their son or daughter and shows the parents that the administration is backing your attendance policy (see Figure 4.10).

MEMORIZATION DEADLINES

Another important factor in your scheduling and timing is memorization of lines (and music during a musical). Again, I have heard horror stories about actors still using scripts at the final dress rehearsal. If this is happening, then you are teaching your students nothing about theatre.

I have found that by setting aside a "Memorization Week" more can be accomplished at rehearsals. Once the cast is announced, a meeting is held to explain what is expected, to take measurements for costumes, and to distribute scripts. Rehearsals then begin exactly one week from this meeting. The week between is used to memorize all lines.

Memorization deadlines should be announced during auditions, allowing students to plan ahead and know what is expected. The key, however, is making the deadlines early and making the students accountable.

In many cases you may require lines to be memorized before that section of the play is blocked. Some argue that it is difficult to memorize lines if the cast has not been blocked through them. From directing over 60 productions, I have found this is not true. Blocking will go smoother and faster if the cast members come to rehearsal with lines memorized.

Furthermore, some directors require that the entire script is memorized before blocking rehearsals even begin. This may sound demanding, but it makes for much easier rehearsals, and students are able to spend more time on character development and less time on line memorization. Again, the key is early deadline. Most people are procrastinators but, when given a deadline, they can be held accountable. Memorization deadlines should be indicated on the Rehearsal Schedule.

LINE CHECKS

Usually there is not time to schedule a separate "line check" rehearsal. However, a student director or another cast member can easily run a line check in the back of the auditorium while you are working with the other cast members on stage.

If a student has the responsibility for line checks, provide a form so that you are aware of which cast members are meeting their deadlines and which are not. Again, making students accountable for their deadlines is important (see Figure 4.11).

Another way to have a fast line check of the entire cast is to have students form a circle. The character who has the first line begins. Each character follows with his or her line as quickly as he or she can say it. This is for line memorization only. Students should not be concerned with characters or delivery, but only with repeating their lines *word for word* in the order in which they appear in the script.

CASTING SMALL CHILDREN

Many productions have parts for small children in the cast, especially in musicals such as *The Music Man, Carousel, The Bad Seed, The Sound of Music, Annie,* and *Oliver!*

When casting a "family," it is often difficult to cast children who look appropriate in size to the parents. Your best source of children would be the elementary schools within your school district. However, you do not want to have an open call, especially if there are many elementaries in your district. Since children are needed for both singing and acting, contact each elementary music teacher for assistance. He or she will usually be happy to help since, if his or her student is chosen, it is a good reflection on the teacher.

Set a criterion for what you need (e.g., size, singing ability, acting ability, projection, etc.). The elementary teacher can announce his or her own auditions and narrow the students down to a prearranged number or representative from the school. You then have the top students from each elementary from which you cast the children needed for your production.

Cast Announcement Letter

Anytime children are cast in a production, a letter should be sent to every child who auditioned, listing the names of those cast. The letter should be encouraging to all and should state once again the criterion for selection. You might consider offering each student who auditioned a free ticket to the show. This not only helps to ease the pain of not being selected but also assures an additional audience, as most of the parents of these children will purchase additional tickets for their family (see Figure 4.12).

Also send a letter to the elementary principals of each school attended by the children who are cast in the show. This is good public relations and, again, assures an additional audience.

Children's Contract

A contract to the parents of the children cast needs to be sent with the Announcement Letter. The contract outlines the responsibilities of the parents. The director does not want to babysit the children during rehearsals. The parents are responsible for this, along with line memorization, costume construction, and so on. Also offer the parents a chance to decline the participation of their child. (In all of the shows in which I have cast children, never have I had a parent refuse to let his or her child participate.) Figure 4.13 shows a sample children's contract.

Children add much to a production and working with them can be a delight. However, make sure everyone concerned understands the commitment, the same as with high school students. You may need to convince the parents you are not doing them a favor by casting their child. Parents must assume the responsibility.

CALLBOARD

It is important to require only those students who are needed to attend rehearsal. A callboard is useful for posting which scenes will be rehearsed. It is then the students' responsibility to check the callboard and see when they are needed at rehearsal.

A callboard can be a bulletin board in your room or you may simply post notices on a designated door of the theatre or your classroom. Wherever or whatever the callboard is, it must be easily accessible to the majority of the cast and crews.

If your rehearsal period is for three hours but a cast member is needed only the first hour, then he or she should be excused to leave. This lets the student actor know that you are not going to waste his or her time, and thus you do not expect him or her to waste your time by not attending a rehearsal.

SCENE BREAKDOWN

Once the cast is assembled, it is helpful to give students a scene-by-scene breakdown that designates which scenes they will be needed for. Many times the script will not indicate a character because he or she has no lines in that scene. Or perhaps a change will be made in the script, adding characters. The breakdown of scenes helps the students know when they are needed (see Figure 4.14).

Some directors feel that a cast can be successfully assembled through a regular class offered during the day, such as a production or advanced acting class. This is not beneficial to anyone involved and is damaging to the program. First, in this type of situation the cast is limited to those who can schedule the class. Many times this is impossible, so many of your better people are lost. On the other hand, you may get some students who could not schedule any other class and took your production class as a last resort. Now you must battle with their lack of enthusiasm of being in the production.

Second, rehearsals during school time are not as conducive to concentrated work as after-school rehearsals. Students are too busy thinking about that math test or history assignment the next hour to concentrate on rehearsing a production. After-school or evening rehearsal will make for a much more comfortable and relaxed situation because the school day is over until the next morning. Even though it may be possible to conduct most rehearsals during the school day, the final rehearsals must be held after school because the running time of an average production is longer than a regular class hour. This then causes problems with students attending rehearsals because they are not used to working on the production after school.

However, a stagecraft class can very easily build sets during the school day. If well organized with deadlines, a stagecraft class can save a director much after-hours work. You do not need to have a scene shop to teach stagecraft; you only need a few tools and a place to lock them up when not being used. Most schools build their sets on the stage, in an empty classroom, in the boiler room, or in the corner of the gymnasium or cafeteria. I have seen beautiful sets that have been built in no more than a corner of a room.

DEALING WITH OTHER PROGRAMS IN THE SCHOOL

It is important to encourage students who are involved in activities other than theatre and to support them in their endeavors. The time has passed when theatre programs must fight to be better than the music program or the sports program. The adage here is, ''If you can't beat them, join them.'' Make it apparent that your program is as important as any other in the school. However, don't try to give the appearance that you are better than any other program, as this will only cause problems. You can be *as* good and *that* is important.

My productions over the years have always included the star football player, basketball player, track and cross country member, wrestler, as well as head cheerleaders and band members. I supported the students in their other activities and saw the significance of them. They, in turn, always saw the significance of theatre and supported it.

It is important to have the same attitude working with the coaches and other activity advisors. They have always returned that support by attending productions and seeing that students in their program attend play rehearsals.

I once told the football coach of a state contender team that players needed to hurry from football practice to play rehearsal. I found out that the coach felt it was important that his players be involved in theatre, and furthermore, that the coach himself was in plays and musicals during his high school days. I attended games and supported the football team, and the coach attended and supported the play productions.

To keep other coaches and activity advisors informed, it is a good idea to distribute a list of those students cast and serving on crews for your production (see Figure 4.15). This is always appreciated and helps others plan around your rehearsals.

THE CONTRACT

Student contracts are very successful in alleviating most attendance problems. The contract, which lists all of your rules and requirements, is signed by both the student actor and his or her parents (see Figure 4.16). The contract is also the start of making your program as professional as possible. What professional actor, technician, or musician works without a contract?

Each contract must be adapted to your particular program. If a problem arises that is not covered in the contract, write a note to yourself and include it in the contract for your next production. You will reach a point where everything is covered.

It is important for all students in the production (not just the cast members) to sign contracts. Contracts can be divided into three sections: Cast, Crews, and Orchestra Members (as in Figure 4.17). The greatest benefit is the support you will receive from parents. When the parents sign their name, they too are taking the responsibility of seeing that the student attends rehearsal and meets all deadlines. Both the student and parent will know the penalty for not attending rehearsals. If a student misses the allotted number of rehearsals (which should be no more than two) and is removed from the show, but the parents want to fight the issue, you have protected yourself and given your administrator the ammunition he or she needs to support your decision.

The parents also know their responsibility in relation to costume construction if you have them help make the costumes (see Chapter 7). If the parent needs to pay for the rental of costumes, the contract can be written to reflect that.

The best result of the contract is that you can count on 98–100 percent attendance at every rehearsal. It works!

In summary, start each production by being organized for auditions and following that organization throughout rehearsals. By having a cast of dedicated students, your job will be easier and you will look forward to going to rehearsals. You have enough to worry about without having to replace cast members during the run of the show. Again, the word is *organization*.

PERFORMANCE THE MUSIC MAN   MONTH September/October YEAR 1981

SUNDAY	MONDAY	TUESDAY	WEDNESDAY	THURSDAY	FRIDAY	SATURDAY
13	14 Auditions 6:30	15	16 Auditions 3:00	17 Read Through 6:30 - 9:30 Entire Cast	18	19
20	21 Chorus 6:30 - 9:30	22 Blocking 6:30 - 9:30	23	24 Blocking Leads and Small Groups 6:30 - 9:30	25	26
27	28 Chorus 6:30 - 9:30	29 Blocking 6:30 - 9:30	30	1 Blocking Leads and Small Groups 6:30 - 9:30	2	3
4	5 Chorus 6:30 - 9:30	6 Blocking 6:30 - 9:30	7 Small Group 3:30 - 6:00	8 Blocking Leads and Small Groups 6:30 - 9:30	9	10
11	12 Chorus 6:30 - 9:30	13 Blocking 6:30 - 9:30	14 Small Group 3:30 - 6:00	15 Blocking Leads and Small Groups 6:30 - 9:30	16	17

All cast and crew members should check the call-board daily in room 138. Not everyone will be needed at every rehearsal so it is important that you check which rehearsals you are scheduled for. This schedule is subject to change.

FIGURE 4.1 Rehearsal schedule.

PERFORMANCE __THE MUSIC MAN__   MONTH __October/November__   YEAR __1981__

SUNDAY	MONDAY	TUESDAY	WEDNESDAY	THURSDAY	FRIDAY	SATURDAY
18	19 Chorus 6:30 - 9:30	20 Blocking 6:30 - 9:30	21 Small Group 3:30 - 6:00	22 Blocking Leads and Small Groups 6:30 - 9:30	23	24
25	26 Full Rehearsal 6:30 - 9:30	27 Add Orchestra Act I 6:30 - 9:30	28	29 Act II 6:30 - 9:30	30	31 Rehearsal 12:00 - 3:30
1	2 Full Dress 6:30 - 9:30	3 Full Dress 6:30 - 9:30	4	5 Full Dress 6:30 - 9:30	6	7
8	9 Full Dress 6:00 - 10:00	10 Full Dress 6:00 - 10:00	11	12 Final Dress And Parents Night 7:00 - ???	13 Performance 8:00 p.m.	14 Performance 8:00 p.m. Cast Party

All cast and crew members should check the call-board daily in room 138. Not everyone will be needed at every rehearsal so it is important that you check which rehearsals you are scheduled for. This schedule is subject to change.

FIGURE 4.1   Continued.

43

CAROUSEL (Auditions, Rehearsals, Important Dates, Deadlines)

September 14,	3:30–6:00	Auditions
15,	3:30–6:00	Auditions
18,	3:30–5:00	Distribution of scripts and important guidelines
21–27		Memorization Week
28,	3:30–6:00	ACT I Dialogue Memorized
29,	3:30–4:30 (MUSIC) 4:30–6:00 (DIALOGUE)	
October 1,	3:30–4:30 (DIALOGUE) 4:30–6:00 (MUSIC)	
5,	3:30–6:00	
6,	3:30–4:30 (MUSIC) 4:30–6:00 (DIALOGUE)	
8,	3:30–4:30 (DIALOGUE) 4:30–6:00 (MUSIC)	
12,	3:30–6:00	ACT II Dialogue Memorized
		Tickets On Sale
13,	No Rehearsal—See you at the choir concert!!	
15,	3:30–6:00	
19,	3:30–6:00	*No Books.* Music and Dialogue Memorized
20,	3:30–5:30	See you at the orchestra concert!!
22,	3:30–6:00	
26,	3:30–6:00	Add Orchestra, ACT I, Set Finished
27,	3:30–6:00	ACT II
29,	3:30–6:00	Problems
November 2,	6:00–10:00	ACT I, Costume Check
3,	6:00–10:00	ACT II, Costume Check
5,	6:00–10:00	ENTIRE SHOW, Makeup, Hang Drops
9,	6:00–10:00	ENTIRE SHOW
10,	6:00–10:00	Teaser (afternoon)
12,	6:00–10:00	Teaser (afternoon)
16,	6:00–10:00	
17,	6:00–10:00	
18,	2:00 p.m.	Senior Citizens Performance
		No evening rehearsal
19,	8:00 p.m.	CAROUSEL
20,	8:00 p.m.	CAROUSEL
21,	8:00 p.m.	CAROUSEL
23,	7:30 a.m.	Strike Set
25,		Return Scripts and Music

Note: Schedule Is Subject to Change

Material covered at each rehearsal will be posted on the callboard each week.

FIGURE 4.2   Rehearsal schedule.

```
┌─────────────────────────────────────────────────────────────┐
│           DANCERS    DANCERS    DANCERS                       │
│                                                               │
│  PLAN YOUR SCHEDULE AROUND THE FOLLOWING TIMES. YOU WILL BE   │
│  EXPECTED TO ATTEND ALL DANCE REHEARSALS.                     │
│                                                               │
│  This year's choreographer is Mr. Mark Huffman. Mr. Huffman is a Choreographer-│
│  Director at Brigham Young University. He has directed and choreographed│
│  shows that have been performed worldwide. Mr. Huffman will choreograph ALL│
│  of the dances in TWO WEEKS. This is why you may not miss a rehearsal. Plan│
│  Now!!!!!                                                     │
│                                                               │
│  Monday–Friday, November 5–18      7:30 a.m.–8:30 a.m.        │
│  Friday, November 6                3:00–6:00                  │
│  Saturday, November 7              8:00–5:00                  │
│  Wednesday, November 11            3:00–6:00                  │
│  Friday, November 13               3:00–6:00                  │
│  Saturday, November 14             8:00–5:00                  │
│  Special Times During the School Day as Arranged             │
│  Rehearsals as Indicated on Original Schedule                │
└─────────────────────────────────────────────────────────────┘
```

FIGURE 4.3   Dance schedule.

```
                              October 26

TO: Jim Van Goethem, Jim Hall, Rob Velasquez, Mark McIntire,
    David Peters, Margie Dywer, Jim Opelt
FROM: Nancy Kelley, Lighting Director
RE: Tech Meeting Dates

Thursday      Nov. 1     6:30 p.m.    Light Crew Meeting
Saturday      Nov. 3     9:00 a.m.    Set Lights. This will probably take most of
                                      the day, so please plan accordingly.
Monday        Nov. 5     6:00 p.m.    Technical Rehearsal
Tuesday       Nov. 6     6:00 p.m.    Dress Rehearsal
Wednesday     Nov. 7     4:00 p.m.    Dress Rehearsal
Thursday      Nov. 8     7:00 p.m.    Performance
Friday        Nov. 9     7:00 p.m.    Performance
Saturday      Nov. 10    7:00 p.m.    Performance

Members of the Lighting Crew must be present at each of the above dates in or-
der to work the shows. Please note that the crew should report one hour be-
fore show time.
```

FIGURE 4.4 Technical rehearsal.

BOTH STUDENT AND PARENT MUST READ THIS INFORMATION BEFORE AUDITIONING OR APPLYING FOR A CREW POSITION.

DEADLINES
Students must meet all deadlines set by the directors.

MAINTAIN GOOD GRADES
Students are to maintain good grades during their involvement in the show. Rehearsals or work sessions will *not* be an excuse for unfinished homework or not being prepared for any class.

NOT EXCUSED FOR WORK
It should be known that students will *not* be excused from rehearsal or crew work sessions because of outside work. Students must arrange work around the rehearsal schedule. The directors of this show are trying to teach students responsibility. If students choose to be part of this show, it is their responsibility to be available when needed.

COSTUME CONSTRUCTION
Cast members are responsible to construct or pay for the construction of their costumes. Materials will be supplied by the Theatre Department. All costumes become property of the Theatre Department after the production.

Cast members will be expected to bring all of their finished costumes to rehearsal when requested and to treat them as their personal property.

PARENT INVOLVEMENT
Parent support is essential to the success of any production. Parents should be willing to set an example for their child by volunteering to sell tickets, work on publicity, or serve as ushers. Parents are invited in attend rehearsals.

AUDITIONING AND APPLYING FOR A CREW IS EASY
Students should sign up for an audition time or crew position but *not both.* If not cast, students who audition may apply for any remaining crew positions.

Auditioning:

1. Sign up for an audition time. You need to come in only one day. Call backs are usually not needed. Sign up in pairs: male-female.
2. Pick up an audition form in room 609.
3. Complete the audition form, including student and parent signatures, and bring it with you to your audition. *(continued)*

FIGURE 4.5   Audition information.

4. Each audition will last about 15 minutes. Auditions will be *closed*. The audition will consist of reading "cold" from the script; singing a prepared musical selection, not to exceed 1½ minutes in length; and performing a prepared dance, organized movement, or gymnastic routine, not to exceed 1½ minutes. The dance routine may be paired or solo. Students must supply accompaniment, which may be live or taped. A limited number of scripts are available in room 609 for students to check out over night.

Crew Applications:

1. Pick up a crew application in room 609.
2. Complete the form, including student and parent signatures, and return it to room 609.

FIGURE 4.5   Continued.

AUDITION INFORMATION

IMPORTANT INFORMATION FOR *CAROUSEL* CAST, CREWS, AND ORCHESTRA

DIRECTORS/DESIGNERS

James R. Opelt—Director
Texanna Ollenberger—Music Director
Jay Roberts—Technical Director
Greg Ferguson—Orchestra Director
Mary Herbert and Alfie Thompson—Costumers
Trudi Kuehn—Hair Stylist
Mark Huffman—Guest Choreographer (Bringham Young University)

ATTENDANCE POLICY
Attendance will be taken at each rehearsal or work session. Attendance at all rehearsals or work sessions you are scheduled for is mandatory. DO NOT ask to be excused or leave early from or come late to a rehearsal or work session, as the answer will ALWAYS be NO! Students missing more than two rehearsals or work sessions will be REPLACED, regardless of part or crew position. Remember, if you don't like your part, someone else does!!! Work is *not* an excuse to miss rehearsal.

Any student missing a rehearsal or work session beginning October 26 will be replaced, regardless of attendance record.

CALLBOARD
All notices concerning the show will be posted on the door of room 609. It is each student's responsibility to check the board *DAILY*. If you miss rehearsal because you failed to read the callboard, you will be marked unexcused from rehearsal.

MAINTAIN GOOD GRADES
Students are to maintain good grades during their involvement in the show. Rehearsals will *not* be an excuse for unfinished homework or not being prepared for class.

COSTUME CONSTRUCTION
Cast members are expected to construct or pay for the construction of their costumes. Materials will be supplied by the Theatre Department. All costumes become property of the Theatre Department after the production. Cast members will be expected to bring all of their finished costumes to rehearsal when requested and treat them as their personal property.

BY WORKING *TOGETHER*, WE CAN CREATE A PRODUCTION OF WHICH WE CAN ALL BE PROUD.

FIGURE 4.6   Audition information.

CREW APPLICATION FORM (FRONT)

Department Head of Apprentice Application

Departments: Costumes
Props
Lights and Sound
Performance/Student Asst. to the Director
Set/Scene Shop
Make-up
Business Management
Publicity
Artist/Designer

Department Head: Junior or Senior
Apprentices: Sophomore or Junior

★ ★

Name _____ Grade _____ Phone _____

Address _____ Zip _____

Department applying for _____

Position (Head or Apprentice) _____

Theatre Experience (Most recent at top):

Play	Position	Month/Year	Organization

Are there any times during the week or during the course of the play that you are not available? (List specific dates and times)

_____

Have you read and agreed to the commitments as listed on the information form?

_____ Yes

(See back)

FIGURE 4.7 Crew application form (front).

CREW APPLICATION FORM (BACK)

Department Head of Apprentice Application

Answer the following questions with a short paragraph:

1. Why are you interested in this position?

2. What specific goals do you have in mind to improve this department?

_____
Student Signature

I understand the commitments associated with the position for which the above named student is applying and furthermore agree to support him/her if he/she is chosen for this activity.

_____
Parent Signature

FIGURE 4.8   Crew application form (back).

FLOWERS FOR ALGERNON STUDENT INFORMATION

Student Name _____

Address _____ Zip _____

Phone _____

Parent's Name _____

Address (if different from above)_____

★ ★

CLASS SCHEDULE   **ROOM**

    A.M.   _____

    HOUR 1   _____

    HOUR 2   _____

    HOUR 3   _____

    HOUR 4   _____

    HOUR 5   _____

    HOUR 6   _____

    P.M.   _____

_____

Character Name
Crew
Orchestra

FIGURE 4.9   Student information form.

Olathe South Senior High School

Patricia A. All, Principal

Kenneth E. Taylor, Assistant Principal
William A. Floerke, Assistant Principal

Nancy E. Keith, Assistant Principal
Tom O'Dell, Athletic Director

September 25, 1990

Dear Parents,

As you well know, your child has been cast in or assigned to a crew for Olathe South High School's musical production, CAROUSEL. The show will be presented November 19, 20, and 21, with curtain time at 8:00 p.m. each evening.

The administration at Olathe South and the directors of CAROUSEL feel it is a privilege to be a member of this show. We also feel that an explanation of our rehearsal and participation policy is in order.

Rehearsal, for the most part, will be held on Mondays, Tuesdays, and Thursdays from 3:00-6:00 p.m. As we get closer to the performances, rehearsals will be held from 6:00-10:00 p.m.

The part your child is playing or the crew he or she is serving on will determine which evenings he or she attends rehearsal. Students are required to check the callboard daily to see if they are needed at rehearsal.

Students must not make a habit of coming to rehearsal late or asking to leave early. Any student missing more than two rehearsals will be removed from the show. A copy of the information that was given to students concerning attendance is enclosed for your perusal. Also enclosed is a rehearsal schedule.

Parent support is essential to the success of any production. We will soon be contacting you for your help in patron solicitation, selling tickets, and serving as ushers. We trust you will volunteer your services in one of these areas.

We feel our productions are a worthwhile, educational experience for all concerned, and we look forward to your child's participation and your support in making CAROUSEL another successful show.

Sincerely,

Patricia A. All
Principal

Nancy E. Keith
Assistant Principal

James R. Opelt
Director of Theatre

Texanna Ollenberger
Music Director

Jay Roberts
Technical Director

Greg Ferguson
Orchestra Director

Olathe Unified School District # 233 ● 1640 E. 151st ● Olathe, Ks. 66062 ● 913-782-7010

FIGURE 4.10 Attendance letter.

LINE MEMORIZATION CHECK

_____ _____ _____
SHOW   LINES (script pages)   CHECK DATE

Actor or Actress   **Good** **Fair** **Poor**   **Needs work on:**
                                                            (give page numbers of script)

                                             _____
                                             SIGNATURE OF CHECKER

FIGURE 4.11   Line memorization check.

Olathe South Senior High School

1640 E. 151st Street • Olathe, KS • 66062 • (913) 782-7010
James R. Opelt, Director of Theatre

Dear Parents,

After auditioning almost 20 elementary students, Texanna Ollenberger and I have selected those students we feel will fit the openings that exist in the Olathe South High School production of CAROUSEL.

Those students selected are:

Britney Eaton
Joshua Eaton
Karadawn Goyer
Jennifer Oatman
Keith Ollenberger
Mathew Pinsky
Kristen Simpson

I wish we could have used everyone but the number needed was limited. The criteria used in the selection process were singing ability, projection, personality, and size.

We appreciate your support and time in letting your children audition and we look forward to working with them when they become high school age.

If for some reason any of those selected are unable to participate, we will replace them with one of the other students who auditioned.

We hope you make plans to attend the musical, which we feel will be a great night of family entertainment. Enclosed please find a free ticket coupon for those students not selected.

Again, thank you.

Sincerely,

James R. Opelt
Director of Theatre

"Building a Tradition of Excellence"

FIGURE 4.12 Cast announcement letter.

Since your son or daughter has been selected to participate in CAROUSEL, we want you and your child to understand the commitment and responsibility required of you both. Below are listed those responsibilities. Please read them over carefully. If you feel your child can or cannot participate, check the appropriate box below, sign, and return this form to Mr. Opelt at Olathe South High School.

1. Parents must agree to help their child memorize lines and music and to meet all memorization deadlines.
2. Parents must be willing to supervise students at rehearsals and performances. Parents may want to get together and organize a system by which parents take turns attending rehearsal.
3. Parents must see that their child attends all rehearsals they are scheduled for. Rehearsals are usually held on Mondays, Tuesdays, and Thursdays from 6:00–10:00 p.m. Rehearsals for the younger students will be held to a minimum. However, it should be understood that the last two weeks of production will be almost an every-night situation.
4. Parents will be responsible for the construction of or paying for the construction of all their child's costumes. Materials will be furnished by the Theatre Department and become property of the department after the show.
5. Parents may be asked to help with costume changes of their child during dress rehearsals and the nights of the show. Here again, parents can work out some sort of schedule.

Please detach, sign, and return to Mr. James R. Opelt, Director of Theatre, Olathe South High School, 1640 E. 151st St., Olathe, Kansas 66062, by Monday, November 2.

_____ Yes, I understand the responsibilities and commitments and give my permission for _____ to participate in Olathe
CHILD'S NAME
South High School's production of CAROUSEL to be presented November 19, 20, and 21.

_____ No, I do not give my permission for my child to participate. Please replace him/her.

_____   _____
PARENT'S SIGNATURE   DATE

FIGURE 4.13 Children's contract.

SCENE BREAKDOWN   Anything Goes

	I-1	I-2	I-3	I-4	I-5	I-6	I-7	I-8	II-1	II-2	II-3
Gillette	C 3 5				C 11	C	C 14	C 15	C 20 21		C 29
Deaton	C 3 5	C 7	C		C 11			C 15	C	C 22	C 29
Kurtz	C		C		C	C		C	C	C 23	C 29
Deters	C 5	C 7			C			C	C	C 22	C 29
Wolf	C		C	C 10			C		C 19	C	C 29
Pickert	C 5	C			C	C		C	C 20	C	C 29
Kelly	C 5				C			C			C 29
Mounkes	C		C					C	C		C 29
VanFleet	C	S 7						P 15	P 19 21		P 29
Tucker	C 5	C 7	C			C		C 15	C 19 21		C 29
Grinnell	C 5	S 7						P 15	S 19 21		S 29
Norris	C	S 7						S 15	S 19 21		S 29
Mallet	C 5	S 7		S				C	C 19 21	C	C 29
Showalter	C 5	C 7	C		C			C	C 19 21	C	C 29

Code: C = Character   S = Singer   P = Passenger   Numbers = Musical Numbers

FIGURE 4.14   Scene breakdown.

Faculty, Coaches, Advisors:

This week begins musical rehearsals preparing for the November 8, 9, and 10 production.

Rehearsals will be held, as in years past, on Mondays, Tuesdays, and Thursdays from 6:00 to 9:00. I would like your cooperation in seeing that students who are involved in your activity preceding musical rehearsal are encouraged to go directly to musical rehearsal. Also please refrain from scheduling over the rehearsal times.

I have always experienced an outstanding working relationship with you and look forward to your continued support. You can be assured that I am supporting you and your program 100%.

Jim Opelt

Kelly Allen	Melissa Grinnell	Royce Rockel
Debbie Bialek	Scott Haesemeyer	Deb Rollf
Angela Biggs	Jim Hall	Janet Rothers
Tammy Bohrn	Scott Harris	Andrea Rothwell
Darin Boysen	Greta Hartman	Bobbi Sawyer
Linda Braun	Peggy Hertzler	Craig Scott
Melissa Caffery	Heather Hoaglund	Joan Seim
Andy Capps	Jeff Hood	Tim Shadoin
Scott Casey	Thad Howard	Greg Shaw
Lee Chapman	Kathy Kane	Jennifer Smith
Kim Chorny	Donna Lies	Monica Stuffings
Melinda Clark	Shellie Lynn	Ed Tolliver
Lisa Cloud	Mark McIntire	Mary Trausch
David Curry	Shannon Meehan	Dan Treas
Tony Davis	Tye Murphy	Jim VanGoethem
Jodi Dodds	John Nichols	Rob Velasquez
Dan Doherty	Shelly Pattrick	Laura Viets
Michele Driskell	David Peters	Shelly Wiliker
Margie Dywer	Jarette Piel	Jeff Wipperman
Jeff Edwards	Debbie Price	David Wolf
Mike Gerber	Ruth Reimers	Nancy Wolf
David Graves	Shelly Richardson	

FIGURE 4.15   Cast announcement.

"FRANKENSTEIN" CONTRACT

Because the cast for *Frankenstein* is small, it is extremely important that each student cast understands the commitment and furthermore agrees to fulfill the requirements to make this show a success.

1. Cast members must attend all rehearsals.
2. Cast members must remain available if extra rehearsals are needed.
3. Cast members must have all lines memorized, word-for-word, by Monday, March 27.
4. Cast members must give 100 percent during all rehearsals and performances.
5. Cast members must have a good working relationship with the director and other cast members and be willing to give and take constructive criticism.
6. Cast members must agree to construct their costumes and to have a good working relationship with the costumer.
7. Cast members must agree to help with set construction and prop collecting when asked by the director.
8. Cast members must agree to personally sell *30* tickets to the two performances and to favorably advertise the production in every way possible.

I have read this contract and promise to fulfill my obligations to the production of *Frankenstein* as outlined in the above 8 items. I also understand that if the director thinks at anytime I am not fulfilling my obligations, he will have a conference with me that could result in my removal from the show. If this does happen, I understand his decision will be final.

_____   _____
STUDENT SIGNATURE   DATE

I understand the commitments required of the student named above and agree to support him/her in this activity.

_____   _____
PARENT SIGNATURE   DATE

FIGURE 4.16   Play contract.

PLAY/MUSICAL CONTRACT

I, _____, hereby agree to accept the part of
_____ in _____
to be presented _____.

CAST MEMBER:
I agree to attend all rehearsals I am scheduled for, and I will remain at rehearsals until the rehearsal is completed and I am excused. If I must miss a rehearsal because of a legitimate reason, I will contact Mr. Opelt at least two days before that scheduled rehearsal. I understand I am allowed to miss only two (2) excused or unexcused rehearsals. If I miss more than two, I will be replaced. I also understand that work is *not* an excuse to miss rehearsal. I further agree to help with sets, meet all deadlines, and do what is expected of me. I also understand that I am responsible to construct or pay for the construction of all my costumes, with the materials supplied by the Theatre Department. I will bring all my finished costumes to rehearsal when requested and treat them as my personal property. After the production, all costumes become the property of the Theatre Department.

CREW MEMBER:
I agree to attend all work sessions and rehearsals I am scheduled for, and I will remain at them until they are completed and I am excused. If I must miss a work session or rehearsal because of a legitimate reason, I will contact Mr. Opelt at least two days before that scheduled work session or rehearsal. I understand I am allowed to miss only two (2) excused or unexcused work sessions or rehearsals. If I miss more than two, I will be replaced. I also understand that work is *not* an excuse to miss a work session or a rehearsal. I further agree to meet all deadlines and do what is expected of me.

ORCHESTRA MEMBER:
I agree to attend all rehearsals I am scheduled for, and I will remain at rehearsals until the rehearsal is completed and I am excused. If I must miss a rehearsal because of a legitimate reason, I will contact Mr. Miller/Mr. Opelt at least two days before that scheduled rehearsal. I understand I am allowed to miss only two (2) excused or unexcused rehearsals. If I miss more than two, I will be replaced. I also understand that work is *not* an excuse to miss rehearsal. I further agree to meet all deadlines and do what is expected of me. I also understand that much rehearsing will be needed outside of the group rehearsals and agree to rehearse on my own as much as possible.

I HAVE READ AND FURTHERMORE UNDERSTAND THE CONDITIONS AS LISTED ABOVE AND AGREE TO ABIDE BY THEM.

_____   _____   _____
STUDENT SIGNATURE   PARENT SIGNATURE   DATE

FIGURE 4.17   Musical contract.

5
Directing

"Mary played a real nice part." "I'm so glad that John remembered all his lines." "What a miracle it was that we got this play on stage in time." "I'm so thankful that the actors didn't just stand on stage; they moved around a little." How often have we heard comments like this after a high school or even a college performance?

An overworked and overtired play director has indeed done very well in getting the production ready for performance since, oftentimes, the play is an extra responsibility that is added to a full-time teaching schedule and other related supervisory activities. The director is fortunate that student actors can take the time for memorizing lines and simple blocking in addition to their other responsibilities, which include homework in all classes and possibly participation in sports, musical groups, other organizations, and maybe even a part-time job. Still, if educational theatre is going to progress and be the hope and foundation for our commercial and national theatre, we have the obligation of fostering solid principles and creating the highest level performances our students are capable of giving. Hopefully, the mark of achievement and quality will be carried on by our students as they progress into college, graduate school, repertory, or even professional theatre.

In this chapter we will examine the role of student actors and how, through *our* guidance, they can aid in their own development as per-

---

This chapter was written with the help of Mr. Barry Alexander, Director of Theatre since 1976 at The University of Findlay, Findlay, Ohio. Mr. Alexander has acted professionally, directed over 500 productions, and each year conducts one of the most successful high school workshops in Ohio.

formers so that they are not merely playing a part but are actually creating a role—a living human being. More important, each student will grow as a person, developing sensitivity and creativity that can be positive factors in helping him or her cope with the various aspects of life, both as a performer and as a mature adult.

We will first review the basic definition and mechanics of *acting*. Suggestions will be given to the student actor from his or her first contact with the play through performance. An extensive study method that has been used successfully will be analyzed with examples of several characters from different plays. In conclusion, a summary of ideas for the actor to use just prior to the performance will be given. This analysis is intended as merely a brief communication of ideas and examples in action; it does not pretend to be thorough or complete. If further investigation is motivated by this discussion, our goal will have been achieved.

Russian theatre authority, Konstantin Stanislavsky, reminds us that, as an actor, one must "love the art in yourself, not yourself in the art." Personal indulgence must be completely separated from one's creation.

KNOW YOUR CHARACTER

Uta Hagen, famed American actress-teacher, tells us that in the construction of a stage character, your objectives provide a powerful basis. They must be selected with strong, personal identification if "they are to provide a solid foundation for the work on the action."* To do this, students must first learn to know their character. The character's education, environment, background, relationships, experiences, and even his or her fantasies play important roles in giving the actor the tools that are needed to know the many facts that make up the character. Actually, there are many selves within our life and we bring each one out, as needed. This is what must be done in creating a character.

The students' knowledge of literature and history also helps a great deal in creating the "new self" on stage. To make every aspect of the character real, actors must *substitute* similar experiences or feelings. They must draw upon whatever they can grasp to aid in their understanding the plights of the "stage" character. The director can explain

---

*Various quotations throughout this chapter are taken from Uta Hagen and Haskel Frankel, *Respect for Acting* (New York: Macmillan, 1973).

what he or she wants and define specifics about how to attain the goals for the character, but the actors' job is to make the feelings and actions real. Actors have to believe the reality before the character can. This is especially true of young actors who may not have *directly* experienced many things in life. Vicarious experiences, observations, and learned behavior will then be the most helpful substitutes in making the ''present'' real. Even such intangibles as feelings for color, texture, music, and elements of nature can be helpful in creating or understanding a role.

SENSE MEMORY AND AFFECTIVE MEMORY

Two effective aids in achieving reality on stage are sense memory and affective memory. *Sense memory* relates to the actor bringing to life or realistically recalling the five senses—sight, sound, touch, taste, and smell. There is no stereotyped behavior for drunkenness, falling asleep, sipping hot coffee, or feeling cold. Each action must be handled naturally if it is to be convincing.

If the actor's concentration is concerned with creating the sense he is working for, the sense will make the face react of its own accord in the simple and natural way it does in life. The audience will see this in exactly the same way it would if you were being observed offstage doing the same everyday thing.

Affective memory is the recall of psychological or emotional responses of the past. In real life, many times we do not base our actions on merely knowing that they are right or wrong; instead, our emotions take over and make our decisions for us. Therefore, our behavior is *realistic*. This is what must be done on stage. Every action must lead to the end result; we cannot begin with the end because we first have to think and then cope with the action. Overanticipation is quick but false. Things do not work that way in life, and they certainly will not be effective on stage. (Read Julian Fast's *Body Language* for examples of realistic behavior shown through the body.)

Physically, an actor must avoid indulgence and be very selective and consistent in creating a few basic traits for his or her character. Concentration on selected characteristics will be far more successful than trying to do too many things at one time. If Laura in *The Glass Menagerie* is slump-shouldered, hesitant, mousey, and indirect in her eye contact with people, but forgets to limp half the time she is on stage, the character is not going to be believable. It is far better, then, to take a few qualities and master them rather than use each of them only some of the time. As actors become more experienced, of course, they are able to retain and do more. The important thing to remember is that real thinking is vital—before, during, and after action. There must be a specific reason for every movement we make, and there must be a logical destination or goal.

In defining the difference between reality in life and reality in art, Tolstoy said, "Something is added to nature which wasn't there before." That "something" is the artist's point of view and his or her power of selection, which comes *from* life and makes for *new* life. Everything must be done with a sense of immediacy and natural progression. One has to select reality and present it on stage convincingly for the audience to be absorbed and convinced.

> We have to open all our senses and innermost feelings to the extraordinary realities of existence. We have to receive these realities with innocence and freshness, as though we had just been born. To create, one has to take known elements and make something new of them, and as we have only a few hours of compressed life on stage, our creation better count. We must *take* life and *what* we take must have pertinence. A mere imitation of nature in its familiar, daily aspects is the antithesis of art.

> When communicating a character to an audience, an actor has to use his or her subconscious thoughts and memories to personalize everything that the character does in his or her stage life. The sum total of all one's stage actions reveals the character he or she has created.

PREPARING THE ACTOR FOR AUDITIONS

As an actor, one's first contact with a play is when he or she reads it. This should occur prior to auditions. Students should read through the entire play twice. The first time will reveal an overall feeling for the purpose of the play and what the author is trying to say and do; the second reading will familiarize the actor with characters and better prepare him or her for the overall presence of each character. At this point, the director should discuss *his or her concept* of the characters as they relate to the play. A really good play has several possible concepts and designs—all of which could possibly work.

We have viewed over a dozen productions of Thornton Wilder's

Our Town. Although the same script was used, several of the directors discovered shadings and values they wished to emphasize in their individual productions, which in turn gave each production a slightly different slant. It is quite helpful, then, to encourage the actors to discuss these important concepts prior to auditions. It will inspire thinking, questioning, and positive end results. Following this, it is a good idea for actors to practice scenes from the play with each other—even improvising situations to familiarize them with the characters from the play. By doing this, the actors will be much better prepared for the auditions and will be able to evaluate ideas that are demonstrated by the other actors who are auditioning.

In short, an audition should be a learning experience. A good audition is inspiring, encouraging, and electrically exciting for all concerned. Believe me—this experience is needed for the intense work that follows.

OBJECTIVE AND SUBJECTIVE RESEARCH

Objective and subjective research and exploration of the play should continue throughout the rehearsal period. Discussing questions like "What does the play want?" and examining the texture of the play should lead to "real" walking, talking, seeing, hearing, smelling, tasting, touching—and feeling. During rehearsals, actors should, in every respect, be totally professional toward the director, toward fellow actors, and especially toward members of the technical staff, whose work and intense devotion often overshadows the work of the actors. Punctuality at rehearsals is mandatory, along with prompt dependability in meeting all deadlines (see Chapter 4).

The old cliché about "actions speaking louder than words" is quite true. Overzealous actors can often take up valuable rehearsal time— sometimes to the point of pomposity—in theorizing and verbalizing ideas for a character. Don't talk it; do it. That is what rehearsals are for. If you, as the director, like it, keep it in; if it's wrong, let the actor know immediately. In spite of today's changing definitions about certain aspects of the theatre scene, ranging from the job of the audience to that of the actor, one is unmistakably paramount and essential:

The director's style and concept must be followed, and the actor's job is to make it live. It is the actor's job to justify, make throb, and make exist that which the director asks, whether the actor agrees or not. Actors must be flexible enough to go *with* the director.

A talented young actor was working in a college production of *The Man Who Came to Dinner*. He was behind in his line memorization and, therefore, was not ready for further development. The rest of the cast was prepared for depth and detail in both characterization and timing. The director decided to work with the others who had been prompt in meeting their deadlines and who were ready for further character development. After rehearsal, the young actor stormed over to the director and exclaimed, "Too much is happening around me. The butler and maid are reacting, doing double takes, and they have practically taken over. They should just walk in, do what they are supposed to do, according to the script, and walk out or stand quietly." The director's remark was short: "If I want pillars, I'll build them." In the concept of the play, every character was a living human being who had a total purpose for existence. This might differ from another director's feeling, but this director felt that there are no small parts; every character can and must be developed. After the verbal conflict, the director firmly made the young actor aware of *his* responsibility to the play. A positive change was evident the next night and his work matched the performances of the butler and maid, as intended.

CHARACTERIZATION

The most essential aspect of any play is *characterization*. Achieving convincing and total characterization can be likened to diving into a swimming pool: You aren't swimming unless you're moving your entire body in the water; wading or dangling one foot in the water doesn't count. The same thing is evident in acting. Actors should go all the way in realizing and creating a character. Utilizing all the principles mentioned earlier, we endeavor to do two things that have proved to be quite helpful—*breakdown* and *individual character analysis*.

BREAKDOWN

Breakdown rehearsals must be properly handled to avoid a real breakdown on all levels. The purpose is to examine everything an actor is doing on the stage, question it, try it again, and polish it. This relates to line delivery, blocking, reactions, general business, and timing. To avoid excessive confusion, all this is done, of course, after basic blocking and line memorization. In other words, at this point you are familiar with the play and are prepared to question motivation and characterizations as they exist. No major changes are made; explanations are given, improvements in reacting are made, development of stage reality is worked on, and there is a general tightening of business.

These are the most exhausting practices because it takes several good, long rehearsals to do this well. I would suggest that you do not try to breakdown more than one act per rehearsal. Allow yourself time, immediately after each breakdown, to go back over everything so that you can make certain that your actors have recorded and remembered the changes. In the end, these will be your most satisfying and fulfilling rehearsals, which ultimately "make" the play. After all breakdowns are completed, the actors and director know the "why" and "how" of everything related to the play.

INDIVIDUAL CHARACTER ANALYSIS

Individual characterizations are developed and written by each actor following breakdown rehearsals and a personal characterization rehearsal with the director. The actor-director team works on any unique problems and questions aspects of the character and the character's relationships with others in the play. The purpose of the written characterization is to have the actor creatively think out and develop a "total" person who has a past, present, and future. The characterizations are discussed after they are read and are then mounted in the lobby for audience viewing so that playgoers can see the creative effort of the actor in developing his or her role. An outline is given to each actor with the notation that it is merely a guide and can be developed in any way the actor sees fit. Elements to be covered in the written characterization are as follows:

The Conception of Character

A. The character's major drive or goal in life and in the play (his or her "spine")
    1. What does the character *want* most? What are the character's needs and drives? What is the character *doing* in the play?
    2. What is the character willing or able to do to get what he or she wants?
B. The character's background
    1. The character's family (influence, relationship, discipline, af-

fection, rejection, economic status, religious attitudes, health, morals)
   2. The character's innate intelligence
   3. The character's educational background
   4. The character's political and sociological environment (war occupation)
C. The character's adjustments to his or her background and the forces that molded him or her
   1. Social adjustments
   2. The character's marriage, if applicable
   3. The character's vocation and career
   4. The character's emotional adjustments
      a. Immature adjustments
         (1) Adjustments by defense mechanisms: compensation, rationalization, aggression, self-righteousness, masochism, sadism, alcoholism
         (2) Adjustments by withdrawal: negativism, fantasy, regression, suspicion, hostility
         (3) Adjustments by repression: anxiety, phobias, compulsions
         (4) Adjustments by physical symptoms: psychosomatic illness, hysteria
      b. Mature adjustments
         (1) Dealing successfully with one's emotions
         (2) Awareness of self
         (3) Sense of humor

The Project of Character

A. The character's age
B. The character's bodily appearance
C. The character's movements (walk, gesture, character, props)
D. The character's voice (pitch, volume, tempo, quality, articulation, dialect)
E. The character's rhythm (jerky or smooth; volatile or even-tempered)
F. Research (biography, history, paintings, newspaper articles, etc.)
G. Imagination (invention by actor)

The creativity of students in developing written characterizations has been quite exciting and successful over the years. A few examples are cited next in an effort to show the magical variations and possibilities of creating a living character.

Steve Hubbell in *A Streetcar Named Desire* is considered to be a minor role but note the actor's detail in describing Steve's marriage to Eunice:

Steve met and married Eunice upon his discharge which, incidentally, was the result of an attempt to leap overboard during a seizure similar to his first. This breakdown, like the earlier one in New York, is now forgotten; at least he doesn't speak of it to his wife. Eunice is several things to Steve. In the most obvious regard, of course, she mothers and fathers him, but more important to the marriage is the fact that she cannot stop worrying about his cheating. Steve, in another environment, would not cheat on Eunice at all, in fear of her, if nothing else. But in order to maintain face value in front of Stanley, Steve actually has been carrying on an affair, though it is about 65% talk and 35% action. This affair with the widow's daughter, who conveniently lives in the quarter, is actually the blonde girl whom Eunice is sobbing about in the fight scene; Eunice has imagined so many affairs prior to this one, however, that she cannot even be sure, and Steve is flabbergasted with the accuracy of her accusation-of-the-month. But Eunice does have ears and she is not stupid. Steve went after this blonde only because Stanley wanted him to be a man about something. As a result, Steve has an affair that he didn't really want in the first place. Stanley, since he respects no one, talks freely to Steve about his girlfriend to see Steve squirm in front of Eunice and stand up to her and say, ''Yes, damn you, I do have a girl.''

In her characterization, also from *A Streetcar Named Desire*, the portraying actress opens her lengthy in-depth study with a telling one-paragraph projection of Blanche:

Blanche DeBois has often been described as a delicate moth-like figure; her actions suggest the fluttering of a moth; she speaks softly and flittingly. She moves in graceful, liquid movements. She is delicate, refined, and sensitive. She is cultured and intelligent, a frail creature who would never willingly hurt anyone. Vulgarity and rudeness go against her nature completely. Blanche is dated. Her speech, manners, and habits are ridiculously typical of the traditional southern belle, yet she cannot abandon this sense of herself as someone special, as a ''lady.'' She cannot and will not surrender the dream she has of herself, and even though she wants desperately not to be lonely, it is her clinging to this dream which keeps her loneliness intact.

The role of Jane Seymour in Maxwell Anderson's *Anne of a Thousand Days* is little more than a walk-on with minimal dialogue. The portraying actress summarizes her study of Jane as follows:

In summation, I find that I like best to interpret Jane as a proud, dignified woman. I understand that her pride will present an arrogant assurance of victory in view of her contest with Anne and that we are seeing Jane only from a stranger's eyes in this play. A stranger would most likely not see the kinder, more idealistic Jane Seymour. I wish, nonetheless, for that kindness to be there in some small way because that is one part of a many-faced character which makes the whole in a certain image.

Excerpts from the portraying actress's analysis of Lottie Lacy in Inge's *The Dark at the Top of the Stairs* certainly show evidence of character understanding and compassion:

Lottie Lacy is fortyish and outwardly appears to be a flamboyant, gregarious, happy person. She was raised in a very straight-laced home, where sex was looked upon as evil. She was the oldest daughter and had to care for her younger sister, which is as close as she ever got to being a mother. Religion does not play a very big part in her life, except where there is some spectacular incident such as the Catholics taking over the world, or some little Jewish lady being much happier in the Christian Science Church, and these are just "news flashes."

Her LOT in life appears LACY, but when the lace is removed, the garment is dull and ugly. As an epitaph for Lottie, an appropriate inscription would be, "There will be time to prepare a face to meet the faces that you meet," from *The Love Song of J. Alfred Prufrock* by T. S. Eliot.

An original concept is displayed by the actor as he examines his role of Johnny Pope, a drug addict in *A Hatful of Rain*, in the form of a medical report:

UNITED STATES PUBLIC HEALTH SERVICE CENTER
FOR NARCOTICS REHABILITATION
LEXINGTON, KENTUCKY

NAME: _____John Pope_____   CASE: _____#204811_____

PHYSICIAN: _____R. H. Austin, M.D._____

After a five-page description of the "patient's" physical condition and psychological conditions, the actor summarizes Johnny as follows:

This case is especially tragic because of the patient's background and war record. The patient's addiction seems to possess many of the same characteristics of alcoholism (e.g., the almost paranoiac refusal to recognize and admit that he has a problem). This perhaps suggests that there is more of a similarity between alcoholism and narcotics addiction than was previously thought. His cure seems to be based on several variables: (1) his ability to forget and forgive the past; (2) his ability to settle and live in an area where drugs would be, for the most part, unavailable and where their use would be unacceptable to those around him; and (3) the love and support he will receive from his wife. The patient has expressed a deep and sincere desire to end his addiction, and from my conversations with the wife, I feel that he will receive all the love and security he will need. Therefore, there seems cause for hope of complete cure in his case.

Another actress developed her characterization of Ruth in *The Effect of Gamma Rays on Man-in-the-Moon Marigolds* in the form of an obituary because she felt that Ruth would die within two years. For purposes of brevity, only the opening and closing paragraphs are included here:

OBITUARIES
1186 Bayside Blvd., Brooklyn
BEATRICE RUTH HUNSDORFER, 20, died Thursday, after a long illness. She was born Nov. 19, 1955, in Brooklyn. She was, for a short while, employed by the science office of Eastside High School. She is survived by her mother, Beatrice, and one sister, Matilda. Services will be held Friday, October 3, at two o'clock p.m. at Swain Mortuary. Burial will be in the Restful Days Cemetery. Service and burial will be provided by the state.

Ruth was born at lunch time on a rainy day. Beatrice was at odds with her before she ever saw her. Ruth had changed her dancing legs to varicose legs. Beatrice saw her eldest daughter once and never held her during the six-day stay in the hospital.

Ruth's future is black. At last, when Beatrice is ready to face the world again and gain back some self-respect through Tillie, Ruth kills every hope. She will be entrapped, until death, in the bitterness, hatred and ugliness of her environment. She will be a slave to stupidity.

Death *is* salvation to Ruth. For Ruth was too close to the Gamma Ray. She was mutated horribly and will finally die. But Tillie was just far enough away to become beautiful and sensitive.

The research an actor can do in preparing a role is an individual matter, but there is no end to the questioning, resources, and creating. Uta Hagen as Martha in Edward Albee's *Who's Afraid of Virginia Woolfe?* continually made notes in her script with questions for research and analysis—questions she immediately answered before she went on to others. The famed acting duo Alfred Lunt and Lynn Fontanne actually "created a full mean," clanking glasses and improvising conversation for an *offstage* scene in Chekhov's *The Sea Gull.* The late actor Paul Muni would go and live in the neighborhoods where his characters might have lived for several weeks prior to the beginning of rehearsals. The important thing to note here is that there is no *single* method, but each actor should employ *some* creative method in developing his or her character.

THE PERFORMANCE

The last phase of a play, of course, is the performance. The discipline an actor must display at this time is essential to the success of the production. Zoe Caldwell, during the run of *The Prime of Miss Jean Brodie* in New York, would arrive at the theatre two hours before curtain time, go to her dressing room, put on her makeup and "prepare herself" for her new creation—for each performance is a challenge with new discoveries. As curtain time approached, Miss Caldwell walked out with Jean Brodie totally alive and ready to appear on stage.

To give spontaneity to a performance, an actor has to develop a feeling of immediacy. As the character comes to life, there are things he or she must think about: What did the character JUST do? What is the character doing right NOW? What is the first thing the character WANTS?

The actor must learn to adopt strict rules for himself and his night's work. He must avoid being distracted or disturbed while in the theatre. When in his dressing room, he must enter into his character by transferring all of his personal thoughts, thoughts not even related to the theatre, to the role itself, for here begins the final culmination of his art. He will give another name, another character, his gift of life.

These are some of the essentials with which you can guide your student actors to develop a quality and discipline that will make their peers and audiences respect not only their talents but their work as actors. Each member of the audience takes home something from an experience in the theatre, and therefore becomes a member of the creative time—director, designer, technician, and the actor who isn't just ''playing a part.'' Our overall goal in educational theatre can best be summarized as follows:

> To bring to an audience the revelation of the failings and aspirations, the dreams and desires, the negative and the positive aspects of human beings—this is what we should set as our goal as committed theatre artists. Then we will be respected and have respect for ourselves and respect for acting.

6

Choreographing the
High School Musical

When a director endeavors to produce a musical, one of the major components of the creative process to consider is the choreography. This consists of the dance and physical movement that will help communicate the intent and significance of the musical. A choreographer's function to the creative team is to understand the concepts that the director hopes to convey and to create the visual essence of the director's ideas through dance and physical movement. The ideal situation for a director is to have a choreographer, being a specialist in his or her field, present new ways of conveying the concept through dance in an innovative and exciting manner. In every musical there is a physical quality that must sustain a connecting thread throughout the show. Once the choreographer is aware of this quality, he or she must understand what is to take place with every aspect of the show (i.e., costumes, lighting, staging, and character development) in order to create dance that will be in harmony with the whole production of the musical.

BECOMING FAMILIAR WITH THE SHOW

The first step the choreographer must take is to become familiar with the musical chosen for production. He or she must also gain a clear

This chapter was written with the help of Mr. Mark Huffman, a choreographer at Brigham Young University. Mr. Huffman has choreographed countless high school productions and his university and professional choreography has been seen around the world.

understanding of the style and nature of the piece. For example, *Annie Get Your Gun* is an example of western style, and the nature of the show is wholesome and fun loving. The choreographer should also study a character analysis of the leads, supporting roles, and chorus. This will provide valuable material that will assist him or her when creating the individual dance numbers. If there is an important message that the audience should receive throughout the process and conclusion of the musical, the choreographer must comprehend the nature of the message in order to create dances that will support the purpose of the musical.

A choreographer has various resources at his or her disposal when analyzing a musical. Obtaining the script and any cast recordings that might be available are obvious sources (see Chapter 13). Researching and finding any books that may give insight to the significance of the time period in which the musical takes place is an important source. One choreographer known for doing extensive research into the subject matter of the piece is Jerome Robbins. He spent a great deal of effort researching and reading the history of the village of Anatevka, its people, and their lifestyle before he choreographed a step for *Fiddler on the Roof.*

The choreographer may also witness other productions of the show he or she is working on to gain additional insight that can reveal new ideas and create a breeding ground for his or her own imagination to grow and flourish. These productions may exist in a movie format, performances recorded on video, or even live performances given by other companies (see Chapter 13). Another source of information concerning the show being produced is to find programs or newspaper clippings of reviews and photographs of previous shows in order to gain a sense of what has been done before. The purpose for watching and researching additional performances in not to copy what one may witness but rather to realize the unlimited possibilities and to gain ideas that will give support to one's thinking. Viewing a production created by someone else may also expose trouble spots to watch out for or concepts in choreographing and directing that could have been enhanced to make the show stronger.

MEETING WITH THE DIRECTOR

The director is the driving force behind the creative process of the musical. After the choreographer has a clear understanding of the show, he or she must then meet with the director in order to learn what ideas the director may have about creating and presenting the overall production of the show. This is extremely important because no two productions of the same show will be presented in exactly the same way. The need for consistency is crucial in order to convey anything of value to the audience. The choreographer should work with the director's concepts in order to make the entire musical become a consistent harmonious piece. Once the ground rules are established, a blueprint is created as to the function and purpose of each individual number for which the choreographer is responsible. He or she also becomes aware of the characters of each roles as seen through the director's eyes and how they function in the individual numbers as well as the whole production.

LISTENING TO THE MUSIC

After the choreographer has learned everything possible from the director's point of view, he or she is now able to listen to the music of the play and have a greater insight as to what must happen with each individual piece. The music he or she will listen to may be from recordings of original cast albums; however, one must be careful when studying commercially produced recordings because many times verses, choruses, or dance breaks are omitted from a song in order to make the product more marketable. The choreographer may also obtain the music score and read musical qualities of the song from the written music. No matter how well a person may read music, the ideal situation would be to have a pianist play the score and record the songs in their entirety so that one may have the opportunity to listen to the music in repeated sessions and gain a full comprehension of the musical piece.

By listening and relistening to the show music, the choreographer can start to formulate ideas and overall pictures for each dance or physical movement. He or she can start to entertain as many ideas as possible and explore all avenues of creativity in developing the dances. The choreographer must understand that all ideas are important and should be examined as possibilities. Even the worst idea, which obviously cannot be used for one reason or another, is valuable because it may point the imagination in the direction that will help the individual discover innovative and exciting approaches to a musical number. By listening to the music and letting the mind be free to consider all possibilities, a person starts to see the overall picture. After entertaining as many ideas as possible, the choreographer must pinpoint and bring into clear focus which movement ideas will work the best in order to convey the director's intent.

PERFORMANCE SPACE

Hopefully, through the previous discussion with the director, the choreographer has gained knowledge as to the type of performing space in which the musical will be presented. The choreographer is now able to examine the performing space with his or her movement ideas in mind to see if both are compatible. Whether choreographing in the round, on a thrust, or on a Proscenium stage, the choreographer must picture the potential of his or her dances as seen by a viewing audience. It is important to keep an open mind because each performing space is unique in presenting challenges that can be used to his or her advantage. If the choreographer is willing to customize movement for the particular performing space and take advantage of what the performing space has to offer, he or she will be able to create new dances to an already familiar musical and give the production an exciting vitality. This is a case of capitalizing on the performing space's strengths rather than exposing its weaknesses.

WORKING WITH OTHER DIRECTORS

After examining the performing space and receiving confirmation as to whether the dance ideas will work or not, the choreographer should have a clear idea of what direction he or she would like to see the dances travel. The choreographer should then meet again with the director to discuss his or her ideas to keep the lines of communication open, foresee any problems that may arise, and receive any recommendations that the director may want to share.

Once the confirmation of his or her movement ideas have been received from the overall director, the choreographer must meet with the musical director, vocal director, stage designer, lighting designer, and costumer. The theatrical process is a collaborative process with all the people involved. The choreographer should discuss ideas with these people in order to elicit any help they may be able to give through their respective creative roles. For example, if your choreographic ideas require a spacial stage construction, the stage designer must be aware of it. The idea you hope to create into a visible dance may not even be possible due to space, budget, and so on. On the other hand, your idea may be entirely possible, and the stage designer may be able to use his or her expertise not only to create your idea through stage construction but also to enhance it in a way that surpasses what you thought could be possible. The same type of meeting, communicating, and collaborating is important with every aspect of the show if one hopes to create the most possible out of the given time, talent, space, and money. The choreographer should always remember that unless other arrangements have been made, the director is the final decision maker. He or she is responsible for the entire production being a success or failure.

After discussing and sharing ideas with the other members of the creative team, the choreographer may come away with a much clearer image of what he or she wants to create. He or she may also discover a whole new approach to choreography that will surpass what was originally intended. All of this effort takes place before the choreographer creates a single dance step. This is vitally important because the choreographer will know exactly the direction in which he or she is heading, which will save time and energy when working with the dancers. The more information the choreographer can comprehend and pin down before starting work with the performers, the more success he or she will have in creating the dance material. He or she will also be free to make responsible judgments when the unexpected occurs.

WORKING WITH DANCERS

Each musical places specific demands on the dancers. Whether it is the tap experience needed for a musical such as *42nd Street* or the country hoedown of *Seven Brides for Seven Brothers*, each requires specific dance capabilities from the performers for the show to be a success. Since the choreographer has been able to analyze the musical, including its background and style, and has developed ideas concerning the different dances within the show, he or she is now prepared to hold auditions for performers and know what type of talent will be needed to create his or her choreography.

When the director is conducting auditions for the show, the choreographer should be there to assist him or her if at all possible. If the choreographer is not available, auditions could be taped and sent to the choreographer for comments. A person auditioning for a certain part may have a wonderful vocal talent but lack the dance talent required of the roll. Likewise, an individual may be an excellent dancer to fulfill the demands of the physical roll but lack any sense of dramatic timing. At the high school level, the situation is rare when a student is competent in all three areas: singing, acting, and dancing. Therefore the production team must work together for the good of the show when selecting performers rather than to make sure his or her area of direction will be provided with talent. The choreographer must know the technical level of dance training demanded of each character for which the students will be auditioning. He or she must also look for strengths from the students as they audition, which may allow the choreographer to capitalize on certain attributes they possess. Seeing a special talent in a performer (e.g., gymnastics) may help the choreographer create additional ideas that will utilize the strength of an individual or group.

The dance audition process may start with a sign-in sheet where the person auditioning completes a resumé form that asks for general information such as name, address, phone, and so on. It should also ask for specific information concerning what dance training the person has had, what type, and for how long. Another valuable question to ask is whether or not the person auditioning has participated in any sport activity. At the high school level, most students have not had extensive dance training. Activity in certain sports may represent the development of a strong mind-body coordination, which is important when that is the existing level of talent. The form should also ask for any additional physical talent or strengths that might give a choreographer an opportunity to create something unique to the student's ability (see Chapter 4).

When auditioning for high school dancers, the atmosphere should not be a threatening one that could prohibit someone from displaying his or her best talent because of experiencing a high anxiety level created by fear and tension. What is the point? In this situation, you are trying to teach students the joy and magic of musical theatre rather than to eliminate them because they are not accustomed to dealing with the pressures of an audition. If a student has any talent on this level, you, as the director, should want to see even a spark of it and then decide whether or not you are able to bring the student's talent to the forefront of his or her performance. Therefore, the choreographer should try to instill a level of confidence in the individual in order for the student to be able to present his or her best self.

Often a person will hold dance auditions by asking students to perform their own dance routine that they have prepared. This is not always the best way to conduct a dance audition. What usually happens is that the choreographer learns who can choreograph movement on themselves, or who has learned a step from the local dance studio and has been spending long hours practicing and performing it. Usually a choreographer does not have the liberty of time that allows for repetitive rehearsals and compensates for the lack of dance training or natural ability. Therefore, the choreographer constantly finds himself or herself in the situation of working with the natural ability of a performer in its raw form. The dance audition should be designed to bring this out of a performer.

LIST OF MUSICALS

When selecting a musical, you must keep in mind the difficulty of the choreography. Following is a list of 29 musicals with a brief description of what type of choreography is needed and the degree of difficulty.

A Funny Thing Happened: Semi-easy to creat any of the steps but difficult for the choreographer due to the strong sense of timing needed to create the physical movement.

Annie Get Your Gun: Easy because it capitalizes on the rough and ready feel of the west, which can disguise undeveloped talent—especially in men.

Anything Goes: Difficult unless there is an abundant amount of talent in tap dancing. Tap dancing requires a great deal of effort and time to master.

Brigadoon: Semi-difficult due to the Scottish style of dancing required for the show and the lengthy ballet numbers originally created by Agnes De Mille.

Bye Bye Birdie: Easy because it deals with a fifties style of dance, which is easy to learn and is acceptable by an audience in its raw form. It may require more time due to the amount of physical movement in the show.

Camelot: Easy because there is not a great deal of dancing and it only has to convey the essence of a medieval quality. Authentic dancing of the period would be nice but it is not required. In either case, the style is not hard to master.

Carousel: Semi-difficult, not because of any determined dance style but because there are so many large production numbers involving many people.

Damn Yankees: Semi-difficult unless there is a strong female lead in Lola and a strong male partner. The rest of the dancing by the men representing baseball players is easy because of the roughness that can be demonstrated by baseball players.

The Fantasticks: Easy because there is no real dancing and what there is does not require a great deal of technique. However, there is a great deal of opportunity for physical movement, which can be created through improvisation that often gets overlooked.

Fiddler on the Roof: Difficult to reach the full technical dance potential of the piece, semi-difficult to create the proper feeling with less talented dancers, and yet still possible to create an evening that the audience will enjoy with high school students.

Funny Girl: Semi-easy because the dancing does not have to be technically difficult to create an exciting show.

Guys and Dolls: Semi-difficult because the dancing of the Hot Box females is expected to be trite, but the male gangster gamblers must be able to perform such numbers as "Luck Be a Lady" with some degree of developed talent.

Gypsy: Semi-difficult because of working with young kids and still creating the vaudeville quality. June also has a difficult duet with her partner when she has matured and is preparing to leave the act.

Hello, Dolly!: Semi-easy because the dancing does not have to be technically difficult to create an exciting show.

How to Succeed in Business without Really Trying: Easy because the dancing does not have to be technically difficult to create an exciting show.

The King and I: Easy because the dancing does not have to be technically difficult to create an exciting show and yet there is the challenge of working with young children.

Li'l Abner: Semi-easy because the movement has the down-home hillbilly feel, which can capitalize on someone's lack of dance training.

Mame: Semi-difficult, not because of any determined dance style but because there are so many large production numbers involving many people.

The Music Man: Semi-easy because it does not have to hold to any style and one can use the strengths of the performers to create the moments that are danced.

My Fair Lady: Easy because there are not a great deal of dance numbers but rather moments where movement is needed to support and convey the meaning of the song.

Oklahoma!: Semi-difficult because even though the dancing is a western style, which can be forgiving in technical abiltiy, this show demands more expert talent to produce the quality of the dance numbers.

Oliver!: Semi-easy because the dancing does not require technical ability to produce the dance moments.

Once Upon a Mattress: Semi-difficult unless you have a strong dancer to play the role of the Court Jester. He or she should have some dance training to fulfill the role. The rest of the dances can be achieved with coordinated performers.

The Pajama Game: Semi-difficult because the dance moments can really utilize strong technical dancers if they are available; however, dances can be created with less talented dancers with a great deal of success.

Pippin: Difficult because many of the songs require strong dancers to communicate the meaning of the song.

The Sound of Music: Easy because the dancing does not demand a strong technical dancer, but it is difficult for the choreographer to create energy and spontaneity to support the songs.

South Pacific: Easy because the dancing can utilize the rough-toughness of the men and the women are not dancing very much.

The Unsinkable Molly Brown: Semi-difficult because even though the dancing is a country style, which can be forgiving in technical ability, this show demands more expert talent to produce the quality of the dance numbers.

West Side Story: Extremely difficult because the dancing requires strong technically trained performers.

7

Costumes

Costuming is one of the most important elements of a successful production; however, it is almost impossible for the director to give the costumes the time and attention they deserve, especially if the production is a musical. As much time can (and should) be spent on the costumes for a production as on the blocking of the actors. With a little help, however, you can have beautiful period costumes for every production. To get that help, you have two options: renting costumes or hiring a costume designer.

RENTING VS. A COSTUME DESIGNER

If you are in a hurry and if your budget isn't a large concern, you will probably choose to rent costumes. However, renting is not painless. With rental costumes, you must still schedule fittings. There is room for error in the sizes delivered, or the item may not be what you wanted. The rental company will not charge you for their mistakes but you will probably be required to pay for your own. And you may still have to hustle to find something appropriate. Because part of the company's charges are based on the length of time the costume is rented, you may get something you are forced to use, despite its unsuitability, because you do not have time to make changes.

The advantages of finding a costume designer and making your own costumes are many. You will never have to settle for something that doesn't fit your expectations. Also, with every show, you are building a stock of various period costumes. After four or five years, it is feasible that you will be able to costume an entire show by using costumes from previous productions. While collecting things to make the costumes, you are building your supply of raw materials. You not only have ready-made costumes but you have a store of materials just waiting to be put together. That brings up one of the problems of making your own costumes—storage.

It is not uncommon for other schools to ask to rent from your stock. Although it takes some work on the part of the director or the costume designer, renting out costumes is a real budget booster.

FINDING A COSTUME DESIGNER

If the costume designer is in charge of organizing instead of actually making the costumes, help is not hard to find. He or she can be volunteer help, a high school theatre student, or the home economics teacher and class. But ideally, you want to find a costume designer who is willing to devote the necessary time, despite the low pay, because he or she enjoys being a part of the theatre staff. (Many schools offer this secondary job to other teachers.)

Your budget will need to include some compensation for your costumers. You could pay for a costumer with ticket receipts or perhaps a business or private party would donate money earmarked for such use. I found that once the administration saw the results that could be achieved with costumers on the staff, the administration was willing to put the costumers under contract as members of the theatre staff.

If you are fortunate enough to find a costume designer who is interested in the theatre program, chances are you can develop a long-term working relationship that will build up your costume inventory and carry you through many productions.

BUILDING RAW MATERIAL INVENTORY

"Things are seldom what they seem," or so Buttercup says in Gilbert and Sullivan's *Pirates of Penzance*. A costume designer working on a slim budget must maintain that attitude when looking for materials to turn into costumes. Never turn any possible costume material down. An open-weave knit vest sprayed with a metallic silver paint becomes chain mail for *Camelot*. A satin drape becomes a dress suitable for a princess in *Once Upon a Mattress*. A ruffled shower curtain masquerades as a cape and sweeps behind *Mame* as she makes her last dramatic entrance. Figure 7.1 shows examples of some wonderful costumes made of drapery fabrics.

Now that you have a costume designer, you need raw materials for her or him to transform into costumes. A letter sent to parents and patrons will bring numerous donations. Donors will be delighted when their cast-off clothing and fabric make an appearance on stage, especially if it is used in a way they wouldn't have imagined.

After receiving a donation, send a letter of thanks to make the donor feel like a part of the current production and theatre program (see Figure 7.2). In doing so, you are building an audience through costume donations, for you can be assured that the contributors will be in the audience to see what's become of their donation!

Donations and many trips to thrift stores made it possible to make 75 period costumes for *Once Upon a Mattress* for under $500. When visiting thrift stores and garage sales, do not think about what the item is now. Keep an open mind. That square throw pillow might double as a terrific hat. (Sew two of the points together with a tacking stitch. A durable headband laced through the middle will shape the "hat" and keep the remaining points in place down over the ears.) That tablecloth accented with gold thread can be transformed into a jacket fit for a prince.

Thrift stores are also good sources of original clothing from the 1930s, 1940s, and 1950s. And many current styles can be adapted to any period. Specific items you may want to watch for at thrift stores include:

- Clothes
- Old costume jewelry
- Shoes
- Hats
- Gloves
- Curtains, drapes, tablecloths
- Bedspreads, sheets

You will also need fabric and trim. Watch for going-out-of-business sales at fabric stores. Sometimes auctions will sell off a store's complete inventory. This can save you more than 75 percent on such things as trim, buttons, patterns, zippers, and thread. These are the items that quickly devour your entire budget. Buy when you find them at a big discount and use them production after production.

Establish a good relationship with one or two fabric stores. Most will give you a discount once they see the quantity of supplies you buy from them. At least one of your stores should be a part of a chain. Fabric is sold by bolts of 20 to 25 yards. When making 20 to 40 of the same costumes, such as the riding outfits for *Mame,* you may need 200 yards of fabric of the same lot and dye number. A chain store can call its sister stores and often supply you with the quantity of fabric needed. If they can't, you will need to ask them to special order the materials.

You may need to supply your costume designer with a letter that gives him or her authority to charge. Such a letter should be written on school or theatre department letterhead and include the designer(s) name, the school and department name, and the school's tax-exempt number.

PATTERNS

Stock up on basic patterns that can be modified to meet a variety of needs. A good example is McCalls #4097 Raggedy Ann pattern, which comes in small, medium, and large sizes for both children and adults. The pantaloons pattern can serve as the baseball uniform pants for a production of *Damn Yankees,* jodphurs for everyone in *Mame,* and gingham bloomers for the Hot Box Dancers' ''Bushel and a Peck'' number in *Guys and Dolls.*

The tunic portion of the pattern may be used short for blouses, hip-length for chain mail undergarments, midlength and belted for some of the male characters in *Once Upon a Mattress,* and floor-length in a biblical Christmas pageant. We have used the pattern with long sleeves, with or without elastic or fabric wristbands, and short sleeved with the same options.

There are several hints for getting a lot of use from basic patterns:

- Buy several of your favorite patterns in every size.
- Reduce and copy the instructions for each item onto separate sheets.
- Cross out the instructions you won't want to use on this particular style and add your own additional instructions at the bottom.
- Supervise and assist your student costume crew in cutting out the material for all the costumes when you have many costumes to duplicate. This eliminates passing out the patterns and spending excessive time getting them back so the next student can use the pattern.

READING THE SCRIPT

Before going any further, the costume designer will want to read the script, with several colors of highlighters on hand. For example, yellow may signal a new day, and therefore a change of costumes for all characters, and green will remind you that a line of dialogue mentioned a specific color or item of clothing. He or she will also want to mark any costume changes that may require speed or ease, such as ''she enters, removing gloves'' or ''she was seen wearing a red dress.''

Next, the designer will want to make a list of all characters, noting the number of changes for each, any specific items mentioned, and special occasions (such as wedding scenes or formal parties). At this point, the costume designer should write down initial ideas for each costume. This list will be a guide as he or she examines materials on hand and browses through the local secondhand stores.

The best source of ideas is pictures. It is easy to find pictures of the original costumes in theatre books. A picture will also help the parents or seamstress who may not be knowledgeable about stage costumes. Keep a running costume picture file. Anytime I run across a picture of a possible costume, I clip it and place it in the file, arranging the pictures in periods.

In addition to the standard costume history and construction books, pictures can be found on calendars, in costume rental company catalogues, fliers sent out by colleges, advertisements, and even in such magazines as *Time* and *Newsweek*. Over a year's time, a file will grow quickly.

INITIAL MEETING WITH STUDENTS

Before you can make much more progress, you need to see the actors and actresses. It is important to schedule a meeting and measuring session now. By scheduling ''appointments'' with the students during or immediately before and after a scheduled rehearsal, you can take the actors' measurements and note physical characteristics you may wish to keep in mind when choosing costumes. This is also a good time to establish rapport with the students. They will enthusiastically tell you what they hope to wear. Although their preferences are not always feasible or appropriate, this is your chance to explain why it may not be possible.

And sometimes their suggestions trigger an idea for an especially brilliant costume.

When scheduling appointments, allow five to ten minutes per student. You may wish to schedule two at a time and let them take each other's measurements as you record the figures (see Figures 7.3, 7.4, and 7.5).

MAKING THE COSTUMES

The secret to making the costumes is to leave the job up to the individual parents. You will save hundreds of hours and thousands of dollars. I have had over 10,000 costumes made by parents for my various productions; their cooperation has always been great. If parents cannot sew, they will find someone to complete the costume, perhaps a grandmother, aunt, or friend.

Before their child auditions, the parents are told that they are responsible for the construction of the costume (see Figure 4.5 and 4.6). This information is given to the students when they sign up for an audition time. Many times they may have to assume the cost to have the costume made. Again, this is the responsibility of the student and/or parent. It is also important to add something like "After the production, all costumes become the property of the _____ High School Theatre Department" to the student contract (see Figure 4.13).

You have the raw materials, the list of costumes needed for each character, and the sizes needed to create the costumes. You now must start distributing the materials to the students so their parents can begin making the costumes.

As you put together raw materials for the costume, you should record each costume as it is given to the student on a Costume Plan Sheet. The plan sheet provides places for the character/student name, scene description, costume(s) description, and a place for listing shoes, hats, gloves, purse, cane, and so on, if needed by the character. There should also be a place to list the number of the pattern you are using and a space to draw sketches and attach fabric samples (see Figure 7.6).

After the plan sheets are completed, they can be placed in a three-hole binder and taken to the fabric store. Each plan sheet should be followed in the notebook by a Costume Checkout form (see Figure 7.7), which lists the student's measurements and the supplies or costumes already checked out to that student.

Now, put the items you have listed in a bag for the student to take home. Also enclose instructions to the parent (see Figures 7.8 through 7.11) and give a completion date. (Set the date several days earlier than you actually need to see the completed costume.) Make the due-back date very clear to the student; otherwise, the parent may not receive the supplies until the day before the costume is supposed to be ready. The costume designer should also include a telephone number where she or he can be reached if there are any questions.

PARENT WORK SESSIONS

Unless parents have worked with you through several productions, you are going to see a large case of parental jitters when those bags of costume supplies and instructions begin going home. It is then time to schedule a parent work session. This time can be used in several ways.

If you can use the school's home economics department and their sewing machines, schedule an on-site work session and invite parents to bring in the item they are working on if they have questions, or to come in and work on specialty items such as hats or trimming completed costumes (see Figure 7.12).

Schedule your work sessions so that parents are working on the same (or similar) costumes. Perhaps you can set up an assembly line production for chorus or dance costumes. Even parents who do not sew can be involved in cutting out patterns, attaching trim, or ironing seams.

If you do not have access to a sewing room, the costume designer can schedule a question session. Notes can be sent home that say, ''I will be available from _____ P.M. to _____ P.M. on ___(date)___ at _____ to answer any questions you have about construction of your child's costumes. Please bring the materials with you so I can show you what to do.''

DISTRIBUTING READY-MADE COSTUMES

Now that the items that must be constructed have gone home with the students, the remaining costumes will be based on ready-made items. These will mostly be from donations and your thriftstore shopping expeditions. Although you may think you know which items will go to certain characters, distributing these costumes requires another meeting with the students.

Again, schedule appointments before, during, or after their practices. Your schedule should allow 10 minutes or more for minor characters who have few costume changes, whereas major characters will need up to an hour. (The character of Mame, in the production of the same name, required three hours.)

During this series of meetings with the cast members, they will be trying on the things you have selected to be modified into their costumes. If the chosen item fits or can be made to fit, you will need to show the student the changes that need to be made to complete the costume. They may need to add trim or change the hemline of a suit coat to fit the period setting of the play. After you have given the student instructions, write them down for the parent. Using both the visual demonstration and the written instructions will reduce the number of hours you will spend answering questions later. Most of the time, you will be asking the parent to do things even a practiced seamstress wouldn't do to a garment. If the instructions are not clear, the students can show the person working on the costume what you showed them. The instructions will suddenly make sense.

An important thing to remember when planning costumes is that the audience will not be seeing the costume up close. No one is going to know if the hem is a "proper" one. In fact, when using very heavy fabric, such as velvet bedspreads or brocade draperies, zigzag the raw edge to reduce raveling and leave it. It will flow gracefully with the character's movements. Unless the back of a dress will get a lot of stress during a vigorous dance, no one will be able to tell it was fastened with velcro instead of the usual zipper.

To facilitate a quick change, you will often choose to do something a seamstress would see as destructive. For example, you may wish to layer several items of clothing. Don't hesitate to cut the entire length of a turtleneck shirt and reclose it with velcro if it will get the character "to the church on time" for his wedding, dressed properly in his dress shirt (worn underneath, of course) and tuxedo jacket.

During this meeting with the students, hand out as many of the costume accessories—hats, gloves, ties, shoes, jewelry—as possible. The more complete the costume is at this point, the less frantic you will be in the weeks before the show.

Note all these changes and the items sent home on the Costume Checkout sheet (Figure 7.7). You will want to make sure you get everything back, including the trim and scraps of fabric (one of those scraps could turn into a treasure in some future production).

WHEN THE COSTUMES ARE COMPLETED

As the students bring in their completed costumes, be sure you see them—on the student, if possible. Minor mistakes and misunderstandings can be taken care of before they become major. The easiest way to do this is with a costume parade. The costume designer and the director should sit in the theatre, watch the parade of costumes, and make comments or suggestions to one another. The costume designer should make notes of changes that need to be made.

At least one week before opening night, set aside time to sit in the audience and watch a full dress rehearsal. Make notes and watch for things as small as two side-by-side costumes that clash and distract, or a color that makes the main character look a sickly green under the lights, or big problems like entrances not made because a costume change couldn't be made quickly enough. The director may suggest ways to solve the problem, the student may need help in getting the change done more quickly, or the costume designer may have to change the costume. Also list items that are still needed, write down questions to ask students concerning costume items that have been distributed but were not worn, and make suggestions to the students about the way they wear the costume, such as buttoning or unbuttoning their coat.

At best, the costumes will help in creating a time, place, and period for the production. The costumes should make the characters wearing them seem believable. At worst, costumes can ruin the illusion the cast and crew have worked hard to create. If the costume is eye-catching and flamboyant, the character should be the planned center of attention in that scene. If the character blends into or helps to create the background, his or her clothes must help set the tone and the time.

THE STUDENT COSTUME CREW

Many students who do not wish to be in front of the footlights enjoy being a part of the production. Volunteers for the costume crew can do many things to help put the costumes together. If you can select from a number of volunteers, choose the ones who have experience in sewing. It will shorten the time you have to spend giving instructions.

The student crew can cut out costumes, add trim to those that have to be alike, assist the actors during quick changes, distribute the costume packets to the students, and many other things. However, until you have worked with them for a while and they have gained some experience, do not depend on them to get the job done without checking up on them. When they are working on an assignment, you must be available to them.

THE DIRECTOR'S JOB

Although it is in the director's best interest to find qualified help and turn the costuming over to that individual, the director is still in charge of the final product.

Schedule meetings with the designer as soon as he or she has had a chance to read the script. Compare ideas and visions *before* the costumes are made. From time to time, you may need to offer support in dealing with a difficult student, or be on hand to unlock storage room doors. Occasionally, you may need to forgive a student's tardy entrance because the costumer kept him or her longer than planned.

Once the show is over, some directors require the students to clean their own costumes before returning them. This may save money, but it can cause you more work later. I have found it easier to collect costumes the night of the last performance. If students take costumes home, it may be several weeks before you see them again

With the right costume designer and a little imagination, you can have wonderful costumes for very little cost. Always be on the lookout for materials that can be made into costumes, be organized, and plan ahead. The result will be costumes that will add much to the overall look of your productions.

FIGURE 7.1 Costumes made from drapes. (Photos by Terry Evans)

95

GARDNER EDGERTON HIGH SCHOOL

318 EAST WASHINGTON
GARDNER, KANSAS 66030

James R. Opelt
Instructor & Director
913-884-7101

"The Home of The Trailblazers"

Mrs. Thomas Brown
123 Main St.
Anytown, KS

Dear Mrs. Brown,

Just a note to thank you for your recent donation of gloves to the GEHS Theatre Department.

We are always grateful for any and all costumes and props, as we never know what will be needed to complete our next production. Your gloves will certainly be put to good use.

Again, thank you.

                                Sincerely,

                                James R. Opelt
                                Director of Theatre

"Dedicated to the Best in Educational Speech and Theatre"
UNIFIED SCHOOL DISTRICT NO. 231

FIGURE 7.2   Donation thank-you letter.

"FLOWERS FOR ALGERNON" Costume Call—Thursday, February 4

4:15	Shawn Reynolds
4:20	Paul Baylor
4:25	Don Chaffer
4:30	Sarah Blacketer
4:35	Heather Comstock
4:40	Christie Wilson
4:45	Susan Savage
4:50	Elba Ortega
4:55	Marjie Earnest
5:00	Helen Veroone
5:05	Diane Bulan
5:10	Jonna Simon
5:15	Lori Schreiber
5:20	Lesley Beck
5:25	Renee Miller
5:30	Chad Coughlin
5:35	Blake Fortune
5:40	Tim Phillips
5:45	Matt Teel
5:50	Everyone inadvertently left off list

This is the first call. There will be a second call next week.

FIGURE 7.3   Costume call.

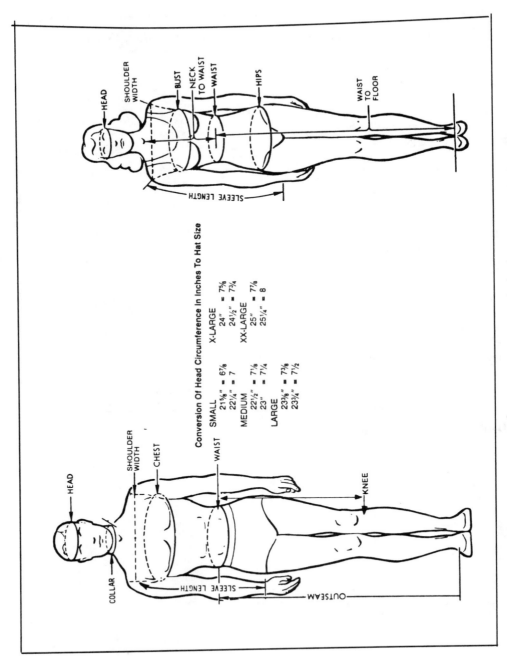

Conversion Of Head Circumference In Inches To Hat Size

SMALL
21⅞" = 6⅞
22¼" = 7
MEDIUM
22½" = 7⅛
23" = 7¼
LARGE
23⅜" = 7⅜
23¾" = 7½

X-LARGE
24" = 7⅝
24½" = 7¾
XX-LARGE
25" = 7⅞
25¼" = 8

FIGURE 7.4   Costume measurement.

SIZE GUIDELINES

Neck (Men's Shirts)
Measure a shirt collar that fits you well. Lay collar flat. Measure from center of collar button to far end of buttonhole.

Chest/Bust (Outerwear, Knitwear)
Measure just under the arms and across shoulder blades holding tape firm and level. Women's measure at the fullest point of the bust and across shoulder blades holding tape firm and level.

Waist (Trousers, Slacks, Skirts, Belts)
Measure over shirt around your waist, where you normally wear trousers or slacks. Hold tape firmly, but not tight.

Hip/Seat
Measure around fullest point of seat while standing. Hold tape firmly, but not tight.

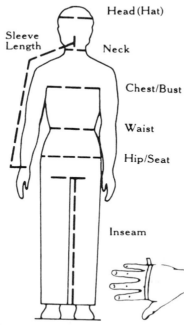

Head (Hat)

Sleeve Length

Neck

Chest/Bust

Waist

Hip/Seat

Inseam

Sleeve Length (Shirts)
With arm relaxed at side measure from center back neck, over point of shoulder, down the outside of the sleeve to the bottom of the cuff.

Inseam
Standing with legs slightly apart measure from the crotch down the inside pant leg seam to the desired length.

Hats and Caps
Measure around the largest part of the head with tape above brow ridges. Convert to hat size using the chart below.

Footwear
Give size and width of dress shoe and/or enclose outline of bare foot.

Gloves and Mitts
Measure around the knuckles with hand flat. (Exclude thumb.) Number of inches equals glove size.

All measurements given in inches.

Convert to Men's or Women's S, M, L, XL sizes or Women's Misses sizes (6-20) using charts below.

***Tall Sizes:** Incorporate additional 1″ in sleeve length and 2″ in body length.

Hat Sizes:	XS		S		M		L		XL		XXL	
Hat Size:	6½	6⅝	6¾	6⅞	7	7⅛	7¼	7⅜	7½	7⅝	7¾	7⅞
Head Meas.:	20½	20¾	21⅛	21½	21⅞	22¼	22⅝	23	23⅛	23⅞	24¼	24⅝

Men's Apparel (Body Measurements)

Size	S	M	L	XL
Neck	14-14½	15-15½	16-16½	17-17½
Chest	34-36	38-40	42-44	46-48
Waist	28-30	32-34	36-38	40-42
Sleeve	32-33	33-34	34-35	35-36

Women's Apparel (Body Measurements)

Sizes	S		M		L		XL	
	6	8	10	12	14	16	18	20
Bust	34½	35½	36½	38	39½	41	43	45
Waist	25½	26½	27½	29	30½	32	34	36
Hip/Seat	36½	37½	38½	40	41½	43	45	47

Sock/Shoe Size Conversion

Sock Sizes	S		M		L		XL	
	8	9	10	11	12	13	14	
Men's Shoe Sizes	1 2	3 4 5 6	7 8	9 10 11	12	13	14	
Women's Shoe Sizes	2 3	4 5 6 7	8 9	10 11	12 13	14	—	

FIGURE 7.5 Size guidelines. (Courtesy of L. L. Bean, Inc.)

COSTUME PLAN SHEET

Page _____

CHARACTER _____   STUDENT _____

Scene/Description _____   Shoes _____

_____   Hat/Hair _____

_____   Accessories (Gloves, Purse, Cane, etc.)

_____   _____

Pattern Used _____   _____

SKETCHES & FABRIC SAMPLES:

FIGURE 7.6   Costume plan sheet.

COSTUME CHECKOUT

Student Name _____ Date _____

Show _____ Performance Dates _____

FEMALE

height _____ insleeve _____ bust _____ waist _____ hips _____

Backneck to waist _____ waist to ankle _____ hat _____ shoe _____

MALE

Height _____ insleeve _____ collar _____ chest _____ waist _____

inseam _____ hat _____ hips _____ shoe _____

Costume Description, Color, Size, etc.	Stock	Borrowed	Date Returned

Pattern #	Fabric	Buttons	Trim

COMMENTS:

FIGURE 7.7   Costume checkout.

MAKING A SACK SUIT (WHERE'S CHARLEY?)

SACK SUIT

You will need a long sleeved shirt with this.

The sack suit was commonly worn in the 1870's. Please alter the suits to look as much like this one as possible. (The audience won't see details. It doesn't have to look good up close.)

PANTS: no cuffs, not baggy, press out center crease.

COATS: hip length, tightly fitted, short, narrow lapels. Button high as possible, sleeve short enough that shirt cuff shows. Curved, not straight in front.

FIGURE 7.8   Making a sack suit—*Where's Charley?*

1892 SLIP CONSTRUCTION (WHERE'S CHARLEY?)

MATERIALS USED:
- 1 fabric strip (for waistband)
- 1 hook and eye or snap
- 3 pieces of nylon net:
  - 1 piece 36 - 40 inches long
  - 1 piece 12 - 15 inches long
  - 1 piece 6 - 8 inches long

1. Fold fabric strip in half the long way.

2. Zig-zag the edges together to prevent raveling. (Edges may be turned under and stiched if machine does not have a zig-zag stitch.)

3. Sew on the hook and eye or snap to fit the waist of the girl snugly. The place where the hook and eye or snap is sewn will be the SIDE of the slip.

4. Tightly gather the longest piece of nylon net in the BACK of the slip. Gather it to about 7 or 8 inches. I find the quickest way to do this is to puch the nylon net together into little pleats and gathers as I sew instead of first putting in a gathering stitch.

5. Gather the second longest piece on top of the first.

6. Gather the third longest piece on top of the second.

The slip will be very full to make the skirt stick out in back.

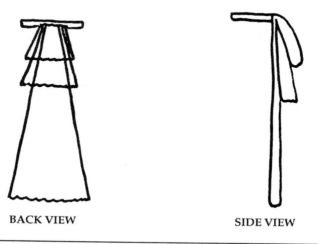

BACK VIEW   SIDE VIEW

FIGURE 7.9   1892 slip construction—*Where's Charley?*

Please read carefully:

- Hair should be up on top of head.
- Hair should be pinned up high in back, "Pompadour" style.
- Lots of curls should frame the face.
- *NO* long hair should be hanging down.
- You will be wearing a hat with your day dress. Bring extra hairpins.
- For "Red Rose Cotillion" you will have silk flowers in your hair—NO HAT.
- We have a hairstyle crew to assist *but* they will be very busy. Please come to *all dress rehearsals and performances* with your hair already up.
- Experiment in advance to see what looks good on you.

FIGURE 7.10   Girls' hairstyles, 1892—*Where's Charley?*

1. Please try to find a costume similar to what is described below. This will help avoid much sewing.
2. Bring what you find to school or practice and have Mr. Opelt or Miss Binger check it.
3. If what you find is a little different than what is listed, bring it in anyway. Perhaps we can make it work with a few changes.

BOYS

Straight-leg jeans
Straight-leg pants of corduroy or colored plain fabric
Shirts—tiny checks, plaids or prints, tiny stripes, plain
Sweaters—vests, V-necked pullovers or cardigans
Sweatshirts or bright colored T-shirts—could be striped but should have no writing
Shoes—white bucks (tie variety) or white tennis shoes; white socks

GIRLS

Pants—solid color (a few could be prints), straight leg, short, zipper in back or on side if possible, tight, a few could be blue jeans
Peddle pushers
Blouses—small collars (round collars best), roll-up sleeves, sleeveless
Sweaters—round neck, some could have collars
Sweatshirts—no writing
Shoes—white girl's tennis shoes, white socks, saddle shoes, brown oxford tie shoes

FIGURE 7.11 Telephone hour—*Bye Bye Birdie.*

Clyde Senior High School

Department of Speech and Theatre

Race Street And Limerick Road
Clyde, Ohio 43410
Telephone 547-9511

JAMES R. OPELT
Instructor and
Director of Theatre

February 15, 1990

We need your help!

As you know, Clyde High School is preparing for its all-school musical "Where's Charley?," and along with the preparations comes the building of over 100 costumes and accessories.

We have tried to do as much as we can with student workers and with sending home other work for parents to complete. But we are to a point that we need more experienced people to help construct hats, parasols, and band uniforms—projects we cannot send home because of detailed instructions.

Many friends and parents have indicated they would be willing to meet together to complete some of the costumes. We have arranged to meet in the home economics room of the high school on Monday, February 26 and Tuesday, March 4 beginning at 6:30. If you could attend one or *both* of these work sessions, it would be greatly appreciated.

Mrs. Walter Binger will lead a group on hats, Miss Binger on parasols, and Mrs. John Jackson Jr. will work on band uniforms.

All you need to bring along is a willingness to work and a pair of scissors. We will have coffee and cookies for everyone. We will attempt to have most of the busy work completed so time can be spent on assembling the costumes.

If you know of someone who would be willing to help, even if they do not have a student involved in the production, bring him or her along!

Thank you for your continued support; it is *greatly appreciated.*

Sincerely,

James R. Opelt
Director of Theatre

Thespian Troupe 2494
chartered April 26, 1979

FIGURE 7.12   Costume work session letter.

106

⑧

Posters, T-Shirts, and Buttons

Advertising your productions is extremely important. If the audience does not know about your event, you may be playing to a very small house. There is no reason high school theatre around the country should by playing to less than 50 percent of its house, yet it is surprising when many high school casts and crews outnumber the audience! Three effective ways of advertising your production are posters, T-shirts, and buttons (see also Chapter 2).

POSTERS

A common mistake when making posters is including too much information. A poster is for quick and easy reference; many times people pass the poster in a storefront. Therefore, the only information that is needed on the poster is the producing company's name (your school), the title and dates of the production, the author's name, the place and time of performances, and ticket information.

The print size should decrease as the importance of information decreases. Be sure to read your royalty contract carefully, as it may state specific requirements for what information and print size must appear on the poster and in all other advertising.

It is not necessary to include the price of the tickets on the poster. If, after reading the poster, people are interested in the show, they will contact the school. Reasonable ticket prices will not keep people from attending the show.

All advertising for a production should be color coordinated and include the same artwork. The colors and artwork should be established at the beginning of the year when the shows are selected. When making your selection, decide on a color that fits the show. For instance, you might use blue for *South Pacific*; red for *Dial "M" for Murder*; red, white, and blue for *The Music Man* or *George M*; gold for *Paint Your Wagon*; or pink and blue for *Seven Brides for Seven Brothers*. These colors should be used for programs, posters, buttons, and T-shirts.

For artwork, you may purchase logotypes from Package Publicity Service, Inc. (see Chapter 14), secure the talents of an art teacher or student, or talk with the school's journalism or publications teacher, who should have books of newspaper slicks that lend themselves well to use on such advertising.

Designing and Printing Posters

Posters can be designed in essentially four ways: student drawn, rub-off letters, offset press, or computer designed.

A good art student can design a very attractive poster. A contest, with the winner receiving tickets to the production, may result in many creative designs. Whoever designs the poster needs to be told by you what information is the most important and what should be emphasized. Have the student make a small sketch of his or her design for approval before making the final copy. Any needed changes can be made before the student puts his or her time into the final design, which should be rendered in black and white. The design can then be easily enlarged or reduced and taken to a print shop that specializes in fast and economical copying (Copies Plus, Kinko's, Quick Print, etc.). The average poster size is 12" × 17".

If you do not have the services of an art student or art teacher, an attractive poster can be made by using rub-off letters and a logo secured from Package Publicity Service or your school's publications' department as mentioned above. The rub-off letters can be purchased from a variety store, drugstore, office business supply store, or through several mail-order companies. Simply place the artwork where you want it and use the rub-off letters to spell out the information you want on the poster. This economical type of poster should also be taken to a local print shop that deals in fast service.

A very professional but more expensive way to have your posters printed is by taking the poster information to an offset press. They will do both the typesetting and printing. Although more expensive, this method will enable you to use color on your poster. Usually, the more colors used, the more expensive. Such printers can be found in the Yellow Pages of the phonebook under "Printers." Plan well in advance if you decide to have your posters printed by this means. Offset presses often require three to four weeks to complete this type of work.

The fourth method, computer designed, is a relatively new way of designing posters. This process usually requires two steps. Most computer designers will design the poster and then subcontract the printing or have you find a printer. The designing can be done quickly but you still have a time problem if you have to wait for a printer. If the poster is computer designed, you may want to make sure that the design company has "in-house" printing available. Again, this process can result in a very professional-looking poster but may be rather expensive. If your poster is very detailed, or if you are going to have a large number printed, or if you have an extensive publicity campaign, computer designing may be your best choice.

To save your budget, you may find a sponsor for the costs of posters (similar to a ticket sponsor, as discussed in Chapter 9). A bank or large corporation makes a good sponsor for such a project. For example, the phone company might provide annual money to underwrite the cost of printing posters. In return, the company can be given an acknowledgment in the program and mentioned in all press releases.

Printing costs and the time needed to complete the print job will vary from printer to printer and sometimes depends on the amount of work a printer has. Make sure you shop around for the best price. Printing costs will also vary depending on the size of the poster, the weight of the paper (card stock is usually used since it will normally stand up in a window), typesetting (unless you have this done in advance), and color and number of inks. Be sure to have all posters printed in the first print run; a second print run could include an additional start-up fee. It is also best to have more posters printed than you may need, as companies charge on a sliding scale in which the more posters you have printed the cheaper the per poster cost is. You will also want extra posters to keep for future reference and students will want posters for keepsakes.

It will also save money and time to have the posters for all your shows printed at one time. This is another advantage of having your season planned in advance. The printing can even be done over the summer. This also allows for faster publicity campaigns. Remember: Preplanning saves you money and time. Figures 8.1 through 8.5 show examples of various styles of posters.

T-SHIRTS

Once you have decided on the poster design, you can easily have T-shirts and buttons printed. The "message T-shirt" has become very popular during the last few years, and you might as well capitalize on this great publicity device. Many companies specialize solely in T-shirt printing. If at all possible, it would be to your benefit to try to use a local printing company since you will have better control of the finished product.

For best results, black print works well on most colors. Again, keep with your color scheme when selecting your shirt. T-shirts do come in different styles, and one type may be more appropriate than another for your purposes. For instance, if you are presenting "Damn Yankees," use a black and white baseball T-shirt. There is no better color than black on white and the baseball-type shirt will complement your publicity campaign.

The design of the shirt should be simple and include only the most important information: the producing organization (your school name), the dates of the production, and the logo you are using on all of your publicity.

The cast and crews should purchase their own shirts. However, you may decide to give away several as prizes when conducting publicity contests. The school secretaries, cooks, and principals should be given shirts in return for a commitment to wear them on specially designated days. During the last two weeks before the play, designate certain days to wear the shirts and then divide the cast and crews and assign them each a day. This guarantees several visible T-shirts advertising the production, walking the halls and community. The shirts also become very visible outside of the school and school district as students travel to various places.

After the production, the T-shirts become souvenirs for the students. Most students continue to wear the shirts long after the production, which sends a message that your department is popular (see Figure 8.6).

BUTTONS

High school students will find that buttons are a fun way to advertise a production. Like show T-shirts, buttons are very popular among high school students and are less expensive than show shirts.

Stock show buttons are available from many different companies. A stock button usually includes the title of the show and some type of caricature. The title and caricature are usually patterned after the original Broadway show design. These will normally be less expensive than a custom-designed button; however, they do not give you individuality. One advantage to stock buttons is that they can be shipped within in a few days, whereas a custom-designed button may take a couple of weeks to be manufactured and shipped. A custom-designed button will cost more but will give your particular show a personalized distinction.

The cost of the buttons depends on the size, artwork, number of different colors used, and number purchased. Again, there are several companies that offer custom buttons for sale. (For more information, see Chapter 14.)

You are free to design your buttons as you want, but it is effective for the buttons to follow closely the design of the show shirt. Buttons are available in many shapes and sizes. A 3½-inch round button works well, as it is not too large to look out of place yet is large enough to include all needed information. The button should include the school name, title of the production, dates of the production, and artwork, or a portion of the artwork used on the program, poster, and show shirt. This provides the continuity in your publicity campaign.

Always distribute the purchased buttons free to the cast and crews first. Many times other students not involved in the production are willing to wear a button and advertise the show. These students can be given buttons after the cast and crews are supplied. Extra buttons can also be used as prizes in connection with publicizing the show or sold to cover the cost of the buttons. Buttons should also be given to the office staff, cooks, principals, and so on, as with the show T-shirts. Students who are not connected with the production yet wear a button emphasize the popularity of the buttons, and they also become a lasting souvenir of the production (see Figure 8.7).

In summary, posters, T-shirts, and buttons are not only great ways to publicize your productions but they are popular with students and the community. Extra buttons and T-shirts can be sold to the audience before and after the show and during intermission at each performance. These forms of advertising become collector items and will be sought after from production to production.

OLATHE SOUTH HIGH SCHOOL

presents

May 6 & 7
Curtain Time
8:00 p.m.

Olathe South High School Auditorium
For Tickets Call:
782-7010 Ext. 32
All Seats Reserved

FIGURE 8.1   Computer-printed poster. (Courtesy of Stan Adell)

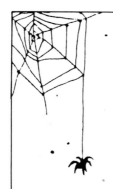

U. S. D. 231
CHILDREN'S THEATRE
PRESENTS

CHARLOTTE'S WEB

by Joseph Robinette
adapted from the book
by E. B. White

Friday, July 6

1:00 pm and 7:30 pm

GARDNER EDGERTON H. S.
AUDITORIUM

FOR TICKETS
    CALL 884−7101 EXT. 210

FIGURE 8.2   Offset poster.

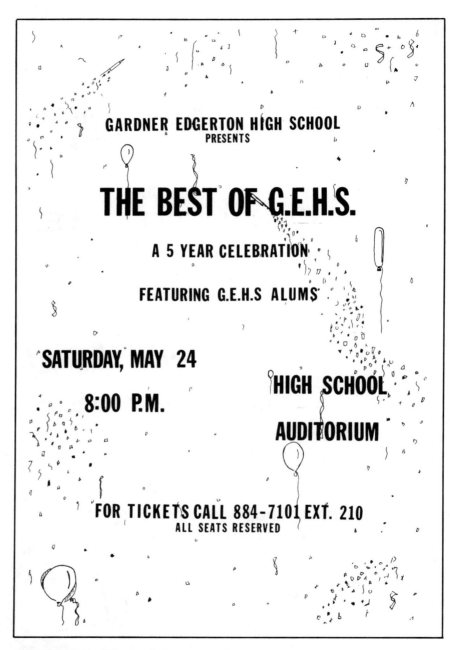

FIGURE 8.3   Student-drawn poster.

FIGURE 8.4 Student-drawn poster, rub-off letters. (Courtesy of Scott Casey)

FIGURE 8.5   Posters. (Photo by Terry Evans)

FIGURE 8.6   T-shirts. (Photo by Terry Evans)

FIGURE 8.7   Buttons. (Photo by Terry Evans)

⑨

Tickets

The printing, selling, and bookkeeping of your tickets is extremely important. The ticket may be one of the first impressions the public has of your production. Time should be spent to ensure that the tickets are printed professionally and sold efficiently, and that clear exact records are kept of each sale.

TICKET POLICY

The first step is to set your ticket policy. This must include a price scale, selling dates and places, and a box-office policy. The ticket policy will alleviate many problems. The following is an effective example:

Tickets for each show will go on sale approximately one month before opening. Tickets to all shows will be sold on a reserved-seat basis. Tickets may be purchased from the Director of Theatre or from the High School office (555-1234, ext. 567).

All tickets must be picked up and paid for at least two days before the performance they are purchased for. No tickets will be held at the box office.

Mail orders will be accepted and filled by return mail if time allows. Payment must accompany the order.

Tickets may not be returned or exchanged.

Do not hold tickets at the box office. When tickets are held at the box office people will reserve tickets and not feel any obligation to attend the performances. If people have tickets in hand they will make a greater effort to attend or will give the tickets to someone who will. Most professional theatres will hold tickets at the box office but require payment in advance. Theatres that do not require prepayment can usually sell the unclaimed tickets easily. At the high school level, however, you don't want just to sell tickets; you want people to *use* them.

ADMISSION PRICES/SCALES

If your season includes a musical and a play, two different price scales are needed. Obviously, a musical is going to cost more to produce, so tickets should be priced higher. The ticket price is also going to send a message to the public of what you think your production is worth. Considering your production is going to be worth the ticket price, make sure you keep your ticket price competitive.

For bookkeeping purposes it is best to have as few different priced tickets as possible for one production. For a musical, I recommend one ticket price for adults and one for students. For a play, one ticket price is acceptable—usually the same as the student musical tickets.

Anyone in a seat must have a ticket. If a parent is willing to hold a child on his or her lap, then the child does not need a ticket. But if that child wants his or her own seat, then a ticket must be purchased. This policy avoids an age cutoff and also helps attract on older audience, thus eliminating young talkers who might interrupt a performance. Of course, I am not suggesting that well-behaved children should not attend the theatre. In fact, I strongly recommend that included in your season is a children's show that is planned especially for the children and focuses on teaching proper theatre etiquette.

Some schools offer reduced tickets in advance of the show. I never found this to be an advantage, however. If you develop an audience, they will purchase tickets in advance based on the quality of the productions, not the ticket price.

RESERVED TICKETS

Reserved tickets make a production appear more professional and it is an easy procedure to set up and operate. Obtain a floor plan of your theatre, showing the location of each seat and its number. A floor plan of your theatre can be copied from the original blueprints used in building your auditorium. If this is not available, you or a student will need to sketch the "house," marking carefully each section, row, and seat. A separate chart is needed for each performance (see Figures 9.1 and 9.2).

Most auditorium seats will already be numbered. If you set up chairs for each production, perhaps in a cafeteria or "gymatorium," you will need to place cardboard numbers at each row. These numbers can be laminated and kept from production to production.

Those people who purchase reserved tickets are able to select their seats from the seating chart. When a ticket is sold, an "X" is placed on the chart, indicating a sold seat. A quick glance at the chart lets you know how many seats are sold for each performance.

Computer programs can be purchased from various companies and will accomplish the same task. The computer programs not only select the best available seats but they also print the tickets as they are sold and store the name and address of the purchaser for future mailings. However, these programs are costly and do not offset their expense unless you do a large number of productions each year. You can set up your own system for little or no cost.

Selling tickets on a reserved-seat basis eliminates students taking tickets and selling them. I have tried distributing tickets to students, and the bookkeeping and control can become very difficult. This is where the use of a ticket order form is necessary.

ORDER FORMS

A ticket order form should include the name of the show, the cost of tickets, and a space for the number of tickets ordered. Also included is a seating preference, ordering instructions, and your ticket policy. You can also add your show logo that appears on your posters and programs. The logo associates the order form with a particular production (see Figures 9.3 and 9.4).

Remember: The order form becomes a record of the sale and gives you the name and address of a future prospective ticket buyer. Keep all ticket order forms and add the names and addresses to your theatre audience records.

FAMILY PLAN

You may want to have a "family plan" for purchasing tickets if your productions cater to families, which most high school productions do. The family plan allows one to purchase tickets for the entire family at a reduced cost. Although this idea is good for public relations, it does cause additional bookkeeping. The family plan ticket order form should include all of the information found on the regular form, with the addition of the family ticket prices (see Figure 9.5).

Each cast and crew member is then given a number of order forms. The students collect orders and bring them to the ticket sellers for filling. Try to avoid accepting ticket orders without money. This rule cuts down on the bookkeeping and also guarantees income.

Once a ticket order is filled, the tickets are marked and sent out with a shortened version of the ticket policy. An example is:

> Please check your tickets to be sure you have received them for the performances you have requested. No refunds or exchanges. All ticket sales are final. No tickets will be held at the box office. Thank you for your support.

Ticket envelopes can be purchased very reasonably from several ticket companies (see Chapter 14). If you decide to use ticket envelopes, purchase the envelopes first. This way, you can have your tickets printed and cut to fit the envelopes, which usually come in only one size.

PATRON, COMP, AND STUDENT ACTIVITY

If you offer free tickets to your theatre patrons, faculty, or staff, mark them such. This can be done by stamping or writing on the back of each free ticket "PATRON" or "COMP" (for complimentary).

Some schools have Student Activity Tickets that students purchase or a Student Activity Fee that students pay. This type of ticket or fee allows the bearer to attend all school activities free or at a reduced rate. If your school has a similar procedure, mark those relevant theatre tickets "STUDENT ACTIVITY." (Custom-made rubber stamps can be purchased at any office supply or printing company.) If tickets are marked in this manner, after the production you can divide tickets by PATRON, COMP, STUDENT ACTIVITY, or regular purchase. You will have an accurate count of how many tickets came through the door and at what price range, which will be helpful in planning future seasons. This information can also be used to figure future royalty costs and, in extreme cases, might be required by the company granting royalties.

BOX-OFFICE REPORTS

It is important to keep clear records of each ticket sale—paid, patron, complimentary, or student activity. For that reason, it is best to have only one or two people handling the tickets and completing daily ticket reports.

It is also a good idea to keep a record of who purchases tickets and their ticket numbers. This is very time consuming, so the use of a computer is advisable. Every show someone will lose his or her tickets and your records will save much time and frustration. If your production is a dinner theatre, keep a record of dinner tickets on the same form.

Overall, two forms are needed to keep track of ticket sales. One form is for the individual ticket sales and needs to include a place for the ticket buyer's name, the production for which the tickets are being purchased, the student or adult price, the ticket numbers, the total cost, and dinner guests if it is a dinner theatre (see Chapter 16). Figure 9.6 shows an example of a dinner theatre ticket form.

The second form is an end-of-the day report. This should include a breakdown of the total tickets sold (student, student complimentary, adult, adult complimentary) and a ticket total. It will also include the total money collected for that day and the total amount banked if this is your procedure for handling money (see Figure 9.7).

PRINTING

Tickets can be printed reasonably and professionally. There are many ticket companies (see Chapter 14) that do very good work; however, having them printed locally allows you to deal with any mistakes that might occur in the printing, and the cost is usually less.

The information to be included on the ticket consists of the producing organization (your school name), title of the show, dates (including the day, month, and year), curtain time, and price scale. Once you have a format established, it is simple to fill in the appropriate information.

Also needed at the right of the ticket is a place for the section, row, and seat. The larger ticket companies will print the actual numbers on the ticket, which will save much time. However, if your house is small, you can do this easily. Figures 9.8 through 9.10 show a number of tickets made by various methods.

TICKET SPONSOR

The more productions you can pay for other than by ticket receipts, the better. I always had a company underwrite the printing cost of the tickets. This is good advertising for the company. By paying to have the tickets printed, the company would have its name and address printed on the back of the ticket. Also include the underwriter in the program acknowledgments and in any press releases (bottom of Figure 9.9).

BOX OFFICE

The box office can easily be handled by parent volunteers. Any tickets not sold in advance will be available at the box office the night of the performance. Tickets are still marked PATRON or COMP, and a final record sheet can be completed for each night's sale.

Some things as simple as tickets can have a lasting impression on your theatre audience. Hopefully, that impression will be one of professionalism, organization, and good management.

Olathe South High School
Auditorium Seating Chart

Production

Performance

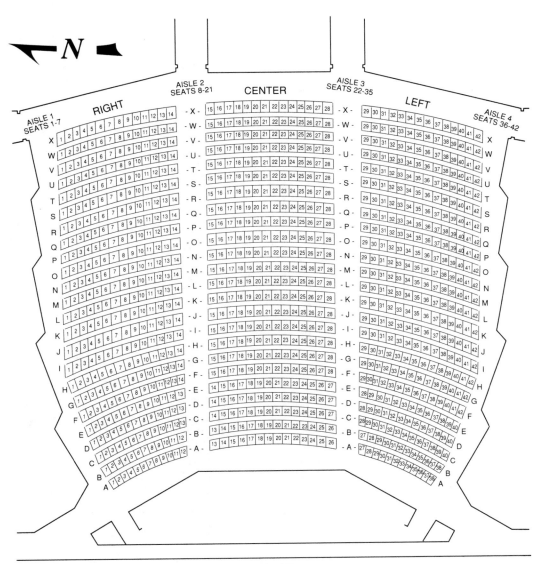

FIGURE 9.1 Auditorium seating chart.

GARDNER EDGERTON
HIGH SCHOOL
AUDITORIUM
SEATING CHART

Performance

Production

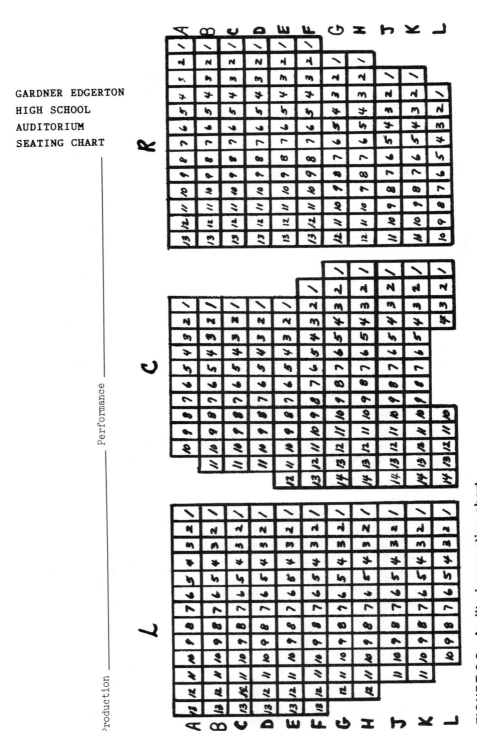

FIGURE 9.2 Auditorium seating chart.

126

TICKET ORDER FORM
Olathe South High School

Please use complete mailing address:

NAME _____   DATE _____

ADDRESS _____

CITY _____   ZIP _____

PHONE _____

Thursday, November 19 – 8:00 p.m.

_____ Adults @ $4.00

_____ Students @ $3.50

Friday, November 20 – 8:00 p.m.

_____ Adults @ $4.00

_____ Students @ $3.50

Saturday, November 21 – 8:00 p.m.

_____ Adults @ $4.00

_____ Students @ $3.50

- -

SEATING PREFERENCE: _____ L _____ C _____ R

All tickets must be paid for and picked up before 11-18-87. Tickets will NOT be held at the box office. No refunds or returns.

PHONE ORDERS: 913-782-7010 Ext. 32 (M - F, 7:30 a.m. - 4:00 p.m.)

MAIL ORDERS: "CAROUSEL TICKETS"
                Olathe South High School
                1640 E. 151st Street
                Olathe, Kansas 66062

FIGURE 9.3   Ticket order form.

TICKET ORDER FORM
Olathe South
High School

Please use complete mailing address:

NAME _____   DATE _____

ADDRESS _____

CITY _____   ZIP _____

PHONE _____

Saturday, December 12 – 1:30 p.m.

_____ All Seats @ $3.00

Saturday, December 12 – 1:30 p.m.

_____ All Seats @ $3.00

- -

SEATING PREFERENCE: _____ L   _____ C   _____ R

All tickets must be paid for and picked up before 11-18-87. Tickets will NOT be held at the box office. No refunds or returns.

PHONE ORDERS: 913-782-7010 Ext. 32 (M - F, 7:30 a.m. - 4:00 p.m.)

MAIL ORDERS: "WE THE PEOPLE" Tickets
Olathe South High School
1640 E. 151st Street
Olathe, Kansas 66062

FIGURE 9.4   Ticket order form.

FAMILY PLAN

Plan	Adults	Students		Save	Total
1	2	2	$12.00	.75	$11.25
2	2	3	$14.50	1.50	$13.00
3	2	4	$17.00	2.25	$14.75
4	2	5	$19.50	3.00	$16.50
5	2	6	$22.00	3.75	$18.25

- -

"SOUTH PACIFIC" Ticket Order Form

NAME _____

ADDRESS _____

PHONE _____

☐ Thursday, March 29   ☐ Friday, March 30   ☐ Saturday, March 31

_____ Adults @ $3.50   _____ Students @ $2.50

FAMILY PLAN

☐ #1 ($11.25)   ☐ #2 ($13.00)   ☐ #3 ($14.75)   ☐ #4 ($16.50)   ☐ #5 ($18.25)

Total Enclosed _____

(Make checks payable to: Clyde High School Theatre Productions)

☐ return to me   ☐ hold at box office

_____

signature

FIGURE 9.5   Family plan ticket form.

FIGURE 9.6 Dinner theatre ticket form.

THEATRE TICKETS
END OF DAY REPORT

Today's Date

TOTAL TICKETS SOLD

Student   _____

Student Comp.   _____

Adult   _____

Adult Comp.   _____

Total   _____

TOTAL MONEY COLLECTED   _____

TOTAL MONEY BANKED   _____

(attach office receipt to this form)

FIGURE 9.7   Ticket end-of-day report.

GARDNER EDGERTON HIGH SCHOOL
presents

Friday, November 11, 1983
Curtain time 8:00 p.m.

Adult $3.50   Student $2.75

Sec.

Row

Seat

TYPESET

GARDNER EDGERTON HIGH SCHOOL
presents

"GUYS AND DOLLS"

Thursday, November 14, 1985
Curtain time 8:00 p.m.

Adult $3.50   Student $2.75

Sec.

Row

Seat

TYPESET

GARDNER EDGERTON HIGH SCHOOL
presents

DIAL "M" FOR MURDER

Saturday, April 4, 1987
Curtain time 8:00 p.m.
All Seats $3.00

Sec.

Row

Seat

TYPESET

FIGURE 9.8   Tickets.

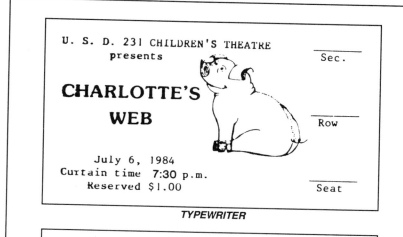

U. S. D. 231 CHILDREN'S THEATRE
presents

**CHARLOTTE'S
WEB**

July 6, 1984
Curtain time 7:30 p.m.
Reserved $1.00

Sec.

Row

Seat

TYPEWRITER

"GUYS AND DOLLS"
Pre-Show Dinner
presented by
Gardner Edgerton H.S. Drama Club
Saturday, November 16, 1985

Dinner served at 6:00 p.m.

Adults $5.75   Children under 12 $3.25

#_____

TYPESET — Dinner Theatre

Compliments Of

FARMERS BANK & TRUST COMPANY
P.O. Box 67
Gardner, Kansas 66030
(913) 884-7715

BACK OF TICKET — Business Underwriter

FIGURE 9.9   Tickets.

COMPUTER

```
         RESERVED

    LFT    T    37


    NOV  17  1988
    OLATHE  SOUTH
    HIGH  SCHOOL
       PRESENTS
    *   *   *   *   *
    *   M A M E   *
    *   *   *   *   *
    OLATHE   SOUTH
    HS AUDITORIUM
      NOV 17 1988
    THU 8:00 PM
    ADULT $4.00

    STUDENT $3.50

    LFT    T    37
       RESERVED


    NOV 17 1988
    *   M A M E   *
    ADULT $4.00
    STUDENT $3.50
```

Olathe South High School
            presents   Sec.____

SEVEN BRIDES FOR SEVEN BROTHERS   Row ____

Friday, February 2, 1990-8:00 p.m.   Seat____
   Adults $4.00   Students $3.50

WORD PROCESSOR

FIGURE 9.10 Tickets.

10
Programs

I look forward to arriving at a theatre production early enough to read the program before the performance begins. Most professional theatres provide a program of some length for the audience to read. You have a captive audience before and during intermission and this is a great time to ''sell'' your theatre department.

Most high schools spend little if any time and expense on printing quality programs. This is another easy task that helps make your production as professional as possible. Ten features should be included in a complete program. These will vary, however, from production to production.

CAST

The cast should always be listed in order of appearance. This allows for easy recognition by the audience. Many times a student's appearance has been changed dramatically to fit his or her character. This type of listing will allow the audience to find its favorite actor or actress. The cast list is a part of the program that audience members will want to refer to several times during the performance. Having the list located in the center of the program will allow it to be found quickly and easily. If your production is a musical, you may want to place a synopsis of the scenes and musical numbers in the center of the program. Most of the audience will want to follow along from scene to scene and musical number to musical number, and consequently will refer to this page throughout the performance. (See the section entitled Musical Numbers and Synopsis.) The cast can then be placed on the first inside page, again for easy reference (see Figure 10.1).

SYNOPSIS OF SCENES

A synopsis of scenes needs to include the time and location(s) in which the action is taking place. This information will always be located in the script, normally at the front or beginning of each scene. A synopsis will help the audience better understand the play and hopefully advance the story (see Figure 10.2 for two examples).

MUSICAL NUMBERS AND SYNOPSIS

If the production is a musical, you need to include the musical numbers and the characters who sing them. Since most musicals will include several scenes and musical numbers, it is best to place this information in the center of the program for easy reference by the audience (see Figure 10.3).

PRODUCTION STAFF

The production staff includes all people (students and adults) on the theatre staff other than cast members. This will vary from production to production, but might include a student director, stage manager, set construction and painting, shift, lights and sound, props, makeup, costumes, ticket reservations, and programs. Also included on the production staff page might be your name and the names of the music director, orchestra director, choreographer, technical director, lighting designer, costumers, and hair stylists.

Another possibility is to list the production staff separate from the adult directors. This would usually be done for a musical since a musical program may need to contain more pages due to the increased information and larger staff. If this separation is done, the names of the directors should appear on the first inside page of the cover under the school's name, show title, and author's name (see Figures 10.4 through 10.6). The section in this chapter entitled Location and Paste-Up discusses this topic further.

DIRECTOR'S NOTES

The addition of director's notes gives your program a professional look and provides credibility to you as a director. Preparing for the notes allows you to do additional research of the show—you may even discover information about the production that you never knew. Items of interest that you find concerning the show when you are planning your season should be filed to use in writing the director's notes.

This information can be found in theatre books or reviews, which are readily available at your local library. Package Publicity Company of New York (see Chapter 14) also supplies information that can be adapted for your notes, along with the descriptions in the play or musical catalogues from which you order the scripts.

Focus on one aspect of the production—perhaps the author, the popularity of the show, the meaning or story line, or performance records (see Figure 10.7).

ACKNOWLEDGMENTS

The acknowledgments may be the most important section of your program. A comprehensive acknowledgments list is great public relations for your department.

Include in this section the names of every person who contributed time, supplies, or free publicity for the production. Keep a running list as the show progresses and add to it as people contribute to the production (see Figure 10.8).

The biggest drawback with acknowledgments is forgetting to mention someone, which can be very harmful. Another problem can be the printer's deadline. Many times it may be necessary to add to the list after the program is printed. This is when a program insert is needed. It normally will consist of a half sheet of paper with additions and/or corrections to the program. Don't be embarrassed to add an insert. I have attended more than 60 Broadway shows and found many program inserts that contained additional information or corrections (see Figure 10.9).

PAST PRODUCTIONS

The audience always appreciates having a list of past productions included in the program. It is fun for the audience members to see how many productions they have seen and, again, it lends credibility to the department by showing the diversity and accomplishments over the past years. The productions should be listed by years in order of the presentation (see Figure 10.10).

MEET THE SENIORS

This section will add a professional look to your program (since most professional programs include a section on "Who's Who in the Cast"). However, because it is time consuming, I suggest you include it only in the program for the final production of the season, unless you have a large staff who can do this for each production.

To assist you in compiling this material, give the seniors a form to complete. Information such as shows the student has participated in, clubs and activities, and graduation plans can then be used to write their individual biographies (see Figure 10.11). Write the biographies yourself or have a third party write them. This way, no student will receive a more glowing biography than another.

If you have a student who writes well, you may want to make him or her responsible for this section. The biographies must be kept short, and each one should begin differently to keep them fresh and interesting. You might also include information about the directors and designers (see Figure 10.12).

PATRONS

When selling patron ads in the program, it is important to proofread them with the utmost accuracy. One of the worst things is to have someone donate money to your department only to have his or her name misspelled or, worse yet, omitted from the program. (More information and an example of the patron layout may be found in Chapter 11.)

MISCELLANEOUS INFORMATION AND POLICIES

Any additional information or policies that you feel your audience should know can be used as fillers. Again, this information will vary from program to program. However, some of this information might include the length of the intermission, picture or record policy, special lobby displays, a dedication, or special thank you's.

The audience will always want to know when and how long intermission will be. Determining the length of intermission will depend on how long the crew and actors need between acts, whether you are offering refreshments for sale, and whether you are having more than one intermission. Selling refreshments can be an additional source of income, but you do not want people bringing food into the show. Therefore, this will take additional policing. Try to keep the break time as short as possible so the show will not lose its flow.

All theatrical programs need a picture and recording policy; in fact, the royalty license may demand such a policy. Taking photographs during a performance can be extremely annoying to other audience members and extremely dangerous to the performers. The final dress rehearsal can be scheduled for this purpose. This "Parents' Night" gives the parents a chance to move around the auditorium, get up on stage, and capture the makeup room activities on film. Of course, the cast and crews should be told in advance to pretend the cameras are not there. If your cast can withstand this evening, they can perform for any audience.

Most royalty agreements prohibit the use of tape-recording devices, video, and film. Make sure to check your contract before arranging any of these.

When providing displays in the lobby for the audience to enjoy before and after the performance and during intermission, indicate in the program who is presenting the display. Invite the art, home economics, and industrial art departments to display their work in the lobby. Lobby displays add a professional touch and, in turn, help to attract a larger audience. Groups or individuals in the community should also be invited to display.

You may have a production that you want to dedicate to a special person or group, or you may have special thank you's that do not fall under acknowledgments. Examples of this miscellaneous information are shown in Figures 10.13 and 10.14.

COVER

The cover may well be the most important part of the program because this is the first thing your audience will see. Always coordinate your posters, buttons, T-shirts, fliers, and programs.

Accompanying the picture should be the school name, title and author of the production, performance dates and curtain time, and place of the performance. Remember: Theatre programs usually become keepsakes. The information you include will not only be appreciated the nights of the performances but for years to come (see Figures 10.15 and 10.16).

LOCATION AND PASTE-UP

One way to cut high printing costs is to have the covers printed professionally and the inside pages of the programs printed in house. A good copy machine can render a nice-looking program and save money. The programs can be paid for in one of two ways: selling ads or patron spots in the program (see Chapter 11), or having a company in the community completely underwrite the cost. This is not hard to accomplish since the company is then mentioned in each of your publicity releases. This is always a good project for the community's large businesses.

If you are doing the layout of the program, it is best to use a computer. Having the program on computer allows you to work and save as you go and to make changes easily as they happen.

The layout of the program depends on its size and length. The directors' and designers' names should appear on the inside cover page or title page. The production title and authors' names should also be included on this page. Many royalty contracts will require an acknowledgment to their company for authorizing the use of the script. This information should also appear on the title page or inside cover (see Figures 10.17 and 10.18).

If there is not enough information to fill every page of the program, the extra page(s) can be used for advertising. The easiest page to ''sell'' is the back cover page since it gets as much attention as the front cover.

If you are unable to sell the space to a local business, use it to advertise your next production or next year's season (see Figures 10.19 and 10.20).

Remember: Your program is important and should be prepared thoroughly and professionally. Programs will become reminders of former productions—make sure they are accurate records.

```
CAST OF CHARACTERS FOR

"ONCE UPON A MATTRESS"


(In Order of Appearance)

Minstrel ................................................................................ SCOTT HAESEMEYER
Wizard .................................................................................... DAN DOHERTY
Princess No. 12 ..................................................................... MELISSA CAFFERY
Lady Rowena ........................................................................ NANCY WOLF
Lady Merrill ........................................................................... DEBBIE BIALEK
Dauntless .............................................................................. GREG SHAW
Queen .................................................................................... LINDA BRAUN
Lady Lucille ........................................................................... DEBBIE PRICE
Lady Larken .......................................................................... LISA CLOUD
Jester .................................................................................... DARIN BOYSEN
Knight No. 1 .......................................................................... TIM SHADOIN
Sir Luce ................................................................................ JARETTE PIEL
Sir Harry ............................................................................... JEFF HOOD
King ....................................................................................... TYE MURPHY
Winnifred .............................................................................. MICHELLE RICHARDSON
Sir Studley ............................................................................ MIKE GERBER
Lady Mabelle ........................................................................ ANGELA BIGGS
1st Lady ................................................................................ JODI DODDS
3rd Lady ................................................................................ SHELLY PATTRICK
Lady H .................................................................................. KIM CHORNY
Knight No. 3 .......................................................................... CRAIG SCOTT
Luce's Lady ........................................................................... SHELLIE LYNN
Omnes ................................................................................... DEB ROLLF
Sir Harold ............................................................................. ANDY CAPPS
Lady Beatrice ........................................................................ JENNIFER SMITH
Sir Christopher ..................................................................... JEFF EDWARDS
Lord Howard ......................................................................... DAVID WOLF
Sir Steven ............................................................................. DAN TREAS
Lady Dorothy ........................................................................ SHELLY WILIKER
Lady Ruth .............................................................................. ANDREA ROTHWELL
Lady Sandra .......................................................................... JOAN SEIM
Lady Martha .......................................................................... LAURA VIETS
Lady Pamela ......................................................................... KELLY ALLEN
Lady Elaine ........................................................................... TAMMY BOHRN
Nightingale of Samarkand .................................................... PEGGY HERTZLER
```

FIGURE 10.1 Cast list.

SYNOPSIS FOR "CHARLEY'S AUNT"

SYNOPSIS OF SCENES

Commemoration Week, Oxford, 1892

ACT I

Jack Chesney's Rooms in College

ACT II

Garden Outside Jack Chesney's Rooms

ACT III

Drawing Room at Spettigue's House

* *

SYNOPSIS FOR "DIAL 'M' FOR MURDER"

SYNOPSIS OF SCENES

The action of the play takes place in the living room of the Wendices' apartment in London.

ACT I

Scene 1—A Friday evening in September.
Scene 2—An hour later.

ACT II

Scene 1—Saturday evening.
Scene 2—Later that night.
Scene 3—Sunday morning.

ACT III

A few months later. Early afternoon.

FIGURE 10.2   Synopsis of scenes.

MUSICAL NUMBERS AND SYNOPSIS
Time: 1873 - 1888

Prelude: An Amusement Park on the New England Coast — May.
CAROUSEL WALTZ ....Orchestra

ACT I

Scene 1: A tree-lined path along the shore — a few minutes later.
JULIE JORDAN ....Carrie and Julie
WHEN I MARRY MR. SNOW ....Carrie
IF I LOVED YOU ....Julie and Billy

Scene 2: Nettie Fowler's spa on the ocean front — June.
JUNE IS BUSTIN' OUT ALL OVER ....Nettie and Ensemble
Reprise: WHEN I MARRY MR. SNOW ....Carrie and Girls
WHEN THE CHILDREN ARE ASLEEP ....Carrie and Enoch
BLOW HIGH, BLOW LOW ....Jigger, Billy and Men
HORNPIPE ....Dancers
SOLILOQUY ....Billy

There will be a ten minute intermission between acts.

ACT II

Scene 1: On an island across the bay — that night.
THIS WAS A REAL NICE CLAMBAKE ....Nettie, Julie, Enoch, Carrie and Ensemble
GERANIUMS IN THE WINDER/STONECUTTERS CUT IN ON STONE ......Enoch, Jigger, Arminy and Ensemble
WHAT'S THE USE OF WONDERIN' ....Julie

Scene 2: Mainland waterfont — an hour later.
YOU'LL NEVER WALK ALONE ....Nettie
THE HIGHEST JUDGE OF ALL ....Billy

Scene 3: Up there.

Scene 4: Down Here. On a beach. Fifteen years later.
BEACH BALLET ......Louise, Young Billy, and Children

Scene 5: Outside Julie's cottage

Scene 6: Outside a schoolhouse — same day.
Reprise:
YOU'LL NEVER WALK ALONE........ Entire Company

FIGURE 10.3 Musical numbers and synopsis.

OLATHE SOUTH HIGH SCHOOL

presents

Music by RICHARD RODGERS
Book and lyrics by OSCAR HAMMERSTEIN II

Directed by
JAMES R. OPELT

Music Director
TEXANNA OLLENBERGER

Orchestra Director
GREG FERGUSON

Guest Choreographer
MARK PAUL HUFFMAN

Technical Director
JAY ROBERTS

Lighting Designer
DAVID MOHLMAN

Costumes
**MARY HERBERT
ALFIE THOMPSON**

Hair Styles and Make-up
DESIGN I

"CAROUSEL" is presented through special arrangement with
THE RODGERS & HAMMERSTEIN THEATRE LIBRARY
598 Madison Avenue, New York, New York 10022

FIGURE 10.4   Musical directors and designers.

PRODUCTION STAFF

Director..JAMES R. OPELT

Technical Director..JAY ROBERTS

Costumes..MARY HERBERT
ALFIE THOMPSON

Programs ....CINDY ASQUITH

Xeroxing...KAY MABERRY

STUDENT CREWS

Assistant to Mr. Opelt..JENNIFER CLINTON
Co-Stage Manager..HEATHER COMSTOCK
Co-Stage Manager..DIANE BULAN
Technical Crew...CONNIE JOYCE
BRIAN MCKINNEY
CINDI THOMPSON
MELANIE SMITH
MELISSA SMITH
Makeup ....KATHY CALORE
JENNIFER BADER
JEANNETTE DARGON
DEBBIE SOLA

FIGURE 10.5 Production staff and directors.

PRODUCTION STAFF

Student Director and Stage Manager ....JOHN BENTLEY

Set Construction ....TED DAVIS
RON LARSON
CINDY THOMPSON
BRIAN MCKENNY
JEROD MILLER
JEFF RHINER
JOSH RUSSELL
RICK WASKOM

Set Crew .... CONNIE JOYCE
ULRIKE KLEIN
JANE LYNCH
DAWN NALL
MELANIE SMITH
MELISSA SMITH

Fly Crew..BRIAN ALTON
JEROD MILLER

Props...MARGO REPINSKY

Light Crew..TREVOR HARBERT
DEBBIE HINZLE
ERIC HITE
JEFF RHINER

Costumes ....MARIA RICHARDSON
JENNIFER RUSSELL

Publicity .... CRYSTAL TOOMAY

Makeup Crew... ELIA ALVAREZ
JENNIFER BADER
TARA STEINBUCH

Carousel Horses .... JIM BRIDSON

Design 1 Personnel ....KAREN ANDREW
THERESA BARB
AUDREA BURTON
TRUDI KUEHN

Programs ....CINDY ASQUITH

Xeroxing .... KAY MABERRY

FIGURE 10.6   Production staff.

DIRECTOR'S NOTES

Pulitzer Prize-winning playwright, Paul Zindel, has created several fine character studies in the three Reardon sisters of "And Miss Reardon Drinks a Little." Through his characters he shows us the self-destruction caused when family members allow problems to pull them apart instead of pull them together.

"In Paul Zindel we seem to have that rarity—a playwright who can write intelligent, sensitive, entertaining plays for a wide public," writes Jack Kroll of *Newsweek*.

"And Miss Reardon Drinks a Little" was a Broadway success starring Julie Harris and Estelle Parsons (Oscar winner for *Bonnie and Clyde*). Performed on Broadway in 1971, the play earned two Tony nominations, one for Estelle Parsons, her third nomination, and one for Rae Allen, also her third nomination. Rae Allen won the Tony that year as best supporting actress.

Our intention is to present good educational theatre to the community. Many ask why we can't just present comedies. You can read comic books all your life or you can read a good novel once in a while. Tonight we present a good novel.

Tonight's production will be the last for three seniors: Linda, Shelly, and Nancy. The leadership, dedication, and energy they have given during the past few years will be missed but never forgotten. I wish them the best of luck as they move on to bigger and better challenges. Thank you for making my life a little fuller—I love you all.

Finally, I would like to thank everyone who has helped to make our season a success. I wholeheartedly thank the supportive parents and friends, businesses, faculty and administration, my Kansas family, my special friend, and, above all, the students who pool their talents to bring you an evening of educational theatre of which we can all be proud.

FIGURE 10.7   Director's notes.

ACKNOWLEDGMENTS

Dr. Pat All
Mrs. Julie Coblentz
Carla Davenport
Forty Winks Sleep Shop, Olathe
Gardner Edgerton High School Theatre
Melissa Howard
Nicole Klarkowski
Mr. Mark Littrell
Mrs. Eileen McDonald—Publicity Pictures
Shauna Michie
Mrs. Peggy Muenks
Olathe North High School Theatre
OSHS Administration
OSHS Custodial Staff
OSHS Faculty
OSHS Secretarial Staff
Radio Voice—Adam Kinzer
Mr. Roger Ramseyer
Mr.David Roberts
Mr. Mike Wallace
Mr. Mark Wilmoth

Special Thanks to All Parents Who Helped with
Costume Construction, Selling Tickets, and
Ushering—Also for Your Patience in Driving
Students to and from Rehearsals and for Making
Sure Meals Were Still Warm Well After the Dinner
Hour. Parent Support Is Vital to Our Success.

Thank You.

FIGURE 10.8 Acknowledgments.

```
SPECIAL THANKS

to

ALFIE THOMPSON

and

MARY HERBERT

and

H.E.L.P. SERVICES

who were inadvertently left off our list of

Special Angels


We apologize for the misspelling of

Mr. Resnick's name.
```

FIGURE 10.9   Correction insert.

PAST THEATRE PRODUCTIONS

1984–85
The Music Man
Our Town
The Matchmaker

1985–86
Anything Goes
Cinderella
An Evening With the GEHS Speech and Drama Dept.

1986–87
Bye Bye Birdie
The Lion Who Wouldn't
Down to Earth

1987–88
Once Upon a Mattress
Sir Slob and The Princess
And Miss Reardon Drinks a Little

1988–89
Guys and Dolls
A Christmas Spectacular
Winnie-The-Pooh
Charley's Aunt
The Best of GEHS

1989–90
Damn Yankees—November 13–15
Clowns' Play—January 14–15
The Desperate Hours—April 3–4

PLAN TO ATTEND
Sr. High Christmas Concert
December 15, 1990—7:30 p.m.

FIGURE 10.10   Past productions.

CAST INFORMATION

_____   _____
NAME   GRADE

_____
CHARACTER OR CREW POSITION

Shows you have participated in:

Cast or Crew   Character or crew position

_____ _____   Anything Goes   _____
_____ _____   Bye Bye Birdie   _____
_____ _____   Down To Earth   _____
_____ _____   An Evening With The...   _____
_____ _____   Once Upon A Mattress   _____
_____ _____   Guys and Dolls   _____
_____ _____   And Miss Reardon Drinks   _____
_____ _____   A Christmas Spectacular   _____
_____ _____   Winnie The Pooh   _____
_____ _____   Sir Slob and The Prince   _____
_____ _____   The Lion Who Wouldn't   _____
_____ _____   Cinderella   _____
_____ _____   Various Christmas Shows   _____

Clubs and activities:

_____ cheerleading   _____ majorette   _____ international club
_____ band   _____ forensics   _____ football
_____ chorus   _____ drama club   _____ basketball
_____ drill team   _____ spirit club   _____ track
_____ volleyball   _____ tennis   _____ science club
_____ stuco   _____ wrestling   _____ cross country
_____ home ec. club   _____ other _____

Opie Awards _____

Briefly explain your after graduation plans. (use back)

FIGURE 10.11   Cast information.

MEET THE SENIORS

DARIN BOYSEN (Jack Chesney).   Darin has played a number of characters during his four years at GEHS. Darin is the winner of two Opie Awards: Newcomer of 1984 and the 1985 Best Supporting Actor Award for the jester in ONCE UPON A MATTRESS. Other credits are BYE BYE BIRDIE, DOWN TO EARTH, GUYS AND DOLLS, student director of AND MISS REARDON DRINKS A LITTLE, and A CHRISTMAS SPECTACULAR, to name just a few. Captain of the wrestling, track, and cross-country teams, Darin has also been involved in drama club, SADD, spirit club, and is president of the student body. Darin has signed a cross-country-track-academic scholarship at Midland Luthern College in Fremont, Nebraska, where he plans to major in communications and education with an emphasis on Radio and TV.

MARGIE DWYER (Stage Manager).   Margie is the most active member of the GEHS Theatre Department. CHARLEY'S AUNT marks her 13th show for which she has served as stage manager. For her work as stage manager, Margie has won three consecutive Opie Awards—the only student ever to do so. Margie is also a member of the concert band, drama club, spirit club, tennis team, and is a majorette for the marching band. Margie is uncertain of her plans after graduation but is considering the fields of broadcasting or business management.

MIKE GERBER (Brassett).   This is Mike's third appearance in a GEHS production, having appeared in DOWN TO EARTH and ONCE UPON A MATTRESS. Mike has been a member of drama club, and the wrestling, track, and cross-country teams. Mike will be attending the University of Kansas on an Air Force ROTC Scholarship in the field of mathematics.

DONNA LIES (Props and Stage Crew).   Donna has been an active crew member, having served on stage, prop, and costume crews for such productions as THE LION WHO WOULDN'T, CINDERELLA, ONCE UPON A MATTRESS, and BYE BYE BIRDIE, among others. She has been a member of band, home ec. club, drama club, spirit club, National Honor Society, international club, and science club. Donna will be attending Saint Mary College and studying to be a mathematics teacher.

DEBBIE PRICE (Donna Lucia D'Alvadorez).   Most will remember Debbie as Adelaide in GUYS AND DOLLS. Her other shows have included ANYTHING GOES, BYE BYE BIRDIE, AND MISS REARDON DRINKS A LITTLE (for which she won the 1985 Opie Award as Best Featured Actress), ONCE UPON A MATTRESS, and

FIGURE 10.12   Meet the seniors.

(continued)

various children's shows. Debbie has also been a member of band, chorus, drill team, forensics, drama club, spirit club, and band. Debbie is undecided as to where she will further her education but is looking toward the fields of broadcasting or travel and tourism.

RUTH REIMERS (Student Director).   Ruth is one of the most versatile members of the GEHS Theatre Department, having served on makeup crew, lighting crew, accompanist for the musical, and having one of the lead roles in this year's production of A CHRISTMAS SPECTACULAR. Her involvement in these various positions has certainly qualified her to serve as student director of CHARLEY'S AUNT, for which she has been nominated for a 1986 Opie Award. Ruth has been a member of concert band, stuco, forensics, drama club, spirit club, tennis, National Honor Society, and drum major for the marching band. Ruth has been accepted at Wichita State to major in oboe performance. But first, Ruth says she hopes to "enjoy my summer the best that I can."

GOOD LUCK. WE WILL MISS YOU.

FIGURE 10.12   Continued.

• •

The artwork in the lobby is presented by faculty members,
Karen McAdoo, Tom Wilson and Dave Kalkman.

• •

SPECIAL THANKS TO:

Continental Telephone Co.
of Kansas
for Posters

Farmers Bank and Trust Co.
for Tickets

Design 1
for Hair Styles

The use of tape recording devices and the taking of flash
pictures during the performances is not permitted.

The audience is invited to remain after the performance
to meet the cast and crew.

FIGURE 10.13   Special recognition.

FIGURE 10.14   Dedication.

GARDNER EDGERTON HIGH SCHOOL

presents
THE SMASH HIT MUSICAL COMEDY

November 13, 14 & 15, 1986

Curtain Time 8:00 p.m.

High School Auditorium

FIGURE 10.15   Cover.

FIGURE 10.16   Cover.

TICKETS NOW ON SALE
GARDNER EDGERTON HIGH SCHOOL

presents

THE MUSICAL COMEDY

GUYS & DOLLS

A MUSICAL FABLE of BROADWAY

Music and Lyrics by
FRANK LOESSER

Book by
JO SWERLING
ABE BURROWS

Based on a Story
and Characters by
DAMON RUNYON

Produced and Directed by
JAMES R. OPELT

Music Director
DOUG BERG

Choreographers
KAREN McADOO
SUSAN SCHUCKMAN

Wardrobe Designer
H.E.L.P. SERVICES

"GUYS AND DOLLS" is presented through special arrangement with
Music Theatre International, 119 West 57th Street, New York, N.Y. 10019.

FIGURE 10.17   Title page.

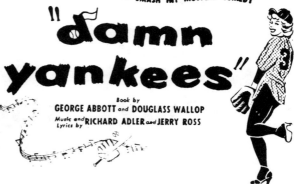

GARDNER EDGERTON HIGH SCHOOL

presents
THE SMASH HIT MUSICAL COMEDY

THE SMASH HIT MUSICAL COMEDY

"damn yankees"

Book by
GEORGE ABBOTT and DOUGLASS WALLOP
Music and Lyrics by RICHARD ADLER and JERRY ROSS

Produced and Directed by
JAMES R. OPELT

Hair Styles
TRUDY KUEHN
TERESA BARB
AUDREA LAQUET

Wardrobe Designers
MARY HERBERT
ALFIE THOMPSON

Music Director
DOUG BERG

"DAMN YANKEES" is presented through special arrangement with
Music Theatre International, 119 West 57th Street, New York, N.Y. 10019.

FIGURE 10.18   Title page.

FIGURE 10.19 Space sold to a local business.

161

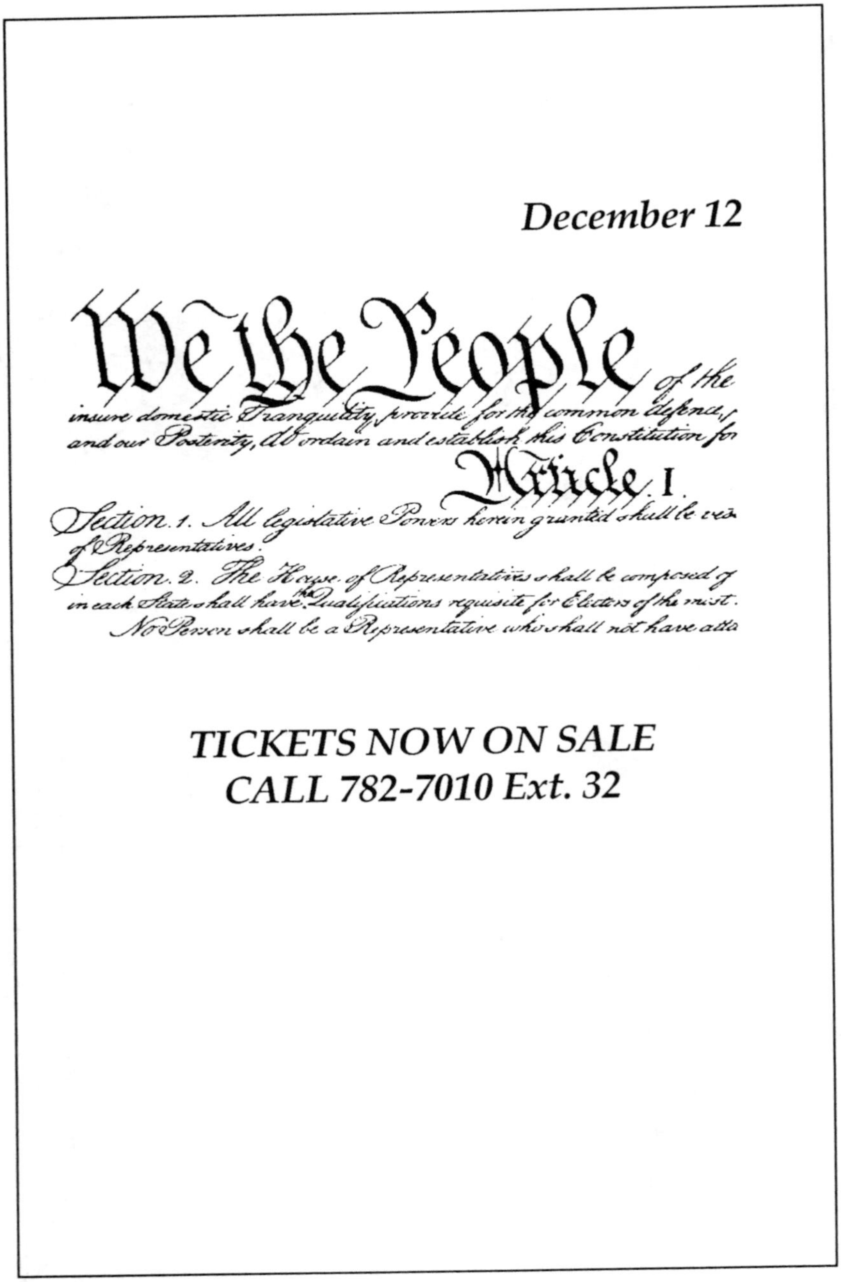

FIGURE 10.20 Advertisement for next production

11

Patrons

No high school theatre department should operate without theatre patrons sustaining its efforts financially. Theatre patrons can contribute thousands of dollars to the theatre department. With the combination of receipts and patron contributions, theatre departments I supervised were self-supporting. Whether your high school's community is 60,000, 6,000, or 3,000, a patron program can be successful. Many of the patrons however, can be out-of-district contributors. The patron money is almost 100 percent profit and, if organized correctly, will require little if any of your (the theatre director's) time.

PROSPECTIVE PATRONS

First, it is necessary to compile a list of prospective patrons. One good source for this is the yellow pages of your local phone book, which list all of the businesses in your district, their addresses, and phone numbers. Generating such a list can easily be done by a student, especially if you are new to the district. Make sure to include doctors and attorneys, as they traditionally will become your best supporters. Next, secure a list, perhaps from your school district's office, of the companies that supply the district. Many of these will probably be out-of-district companies, which will add to your list of prospective patrons. By supplying the district, they will feel obligated and know that it will be good public relations to give some money back to the district—your theatre department will be the fortunate beneficiary.

Another place to check is the school yearbook and/or newspaper to see what companies advertise in these publications. Finally, names and addresses of your students' parents and the district faculty and staff list will provide additional prospective patrons. However, you will find that the best source of new patrons are your current ticket buyers who will pass along the information on becoming a patron.

DISPLAY ADS, NAME LISTINGS, AND BUSINESS CARDS

Once this list is developed, you need to decide what type of advertising or format you will use to list the patrons. Three types are recommended: display ads, name listings, and business cards.

Although the display ad gives your program a professional look, I found that there were several drawbacks to this type of program advertising. First, the time involved is much greater than the name listing. Also, a large program is needed because display ads take up more room. Another disadvantage is that it takes the patrons longer to make up their mind on what to include in the display ad, and you must have personal contact with each prospective patron in order for him or her to explain exactly what he or she wants included. A greater margin of error also exists with the display ad since so much information is involved. When using this method, the printing of the program becomes more costly because you may not have the resources to do such a project in-house.

Anyone with a typewriter and a copy machine can print a professional-looking program using name listings. Although I do not suggest selling ads over the phone or through the mail, you can do this when selling name listings. If you choose to list your patrons by name, you may want to add a paragraph as a heading to the list, thanking the patrons for their support.

Finally, listing patrons by business cards can be both easy and restricting. It is an easy way to list patrons because when they give you their business card, you already have the ad laid out. All you need to do is to arrange the cards on the page and duplicate them. However, this format may restrict those businesses or people who do not have business cards from advertising in your program. Those who do not have cards may have access to ads used in other publications (e.g., the yellow pages) that they will give you permission to use (see Figures 11.1 through 11.5).

SETTING PRICES AND FEATURES

When selling display ads, you need to determine a price per page of the program and divide the ads accordingly. The smaller ads should be priced proportionately higher than the big ads because you will sell more small ads than big ones. Although the size of the overall program is of individual choice, the average program measures 5½ × 8½ inches. This size program would then offer ads that would measure 1/8, 1/4, 1/3, 1/2, and a full page. The respective prices might be $12, $18, $22, $32, and $60. The cost set for the ads should be competitive with today's prices. In setting prices, figure the cost per page to have the program printed. Add a small profit per page and set your ad prices accordingly.

Using name listings results in higher profits and saves time. Consider offering your supporters a choice of four different-priced patron categories: A "Special Angel" sold for $75, an "Angel" for $40, a "Donor" for $30, and a "Sponsor" for $20. If your high school is located in a large city where there is much industry, you may want to add a "Corporate Angel" category for larger companies. A fee of $250 for Corporate Angels would be appropriate.

In addition to raising money, you are trying to attract an audience for your shows. Most people want something for their money, and the best thing you have to give them is tickets. To ensure profits, the total cost of the free tickets needs to be less than the cost of the purchased ad. Another benefit of giving tickets to your patrons is that they usually purchase additional ones.

Tickets and incentives for the patrons might be as follows: Sponsors, one free ticket to one performance of each show of the season; Donors, two tickets; Angels, three tickets; and Special Angels, four tickets and their name on a Special Angels board in the lobby of the auditorium. Corporate Angels might also receive four tickets and their name on a special Corporate Angel board in the lobby.

Prospective patrons should complete a form that includes the information discussed above along with their name, address, city, zip and phone number. It is important to have a current and accurate address for mailing the free ticket coupons. It is also helpful to have an explanation of your patron features to leave with the prospective patron when selling the ad. Examples of a display ad form, name listing form, and patron features flier are shown in Figures 11.6 through 11.8.

PARENT PROMOTIONAL COMMITTEE

It is necessary to form a committee to canvass the community to collect patrons. Having used both students and parents on such committees I have found the parent group much more workable. Students have enough to do attending rehearsals and memorizing lines, dances, and songs, along with homework and other school activities. Therefore, this is a great opportunity to involve parents. They are better able to talk businesses into becoming patrons because the parents may be business-people themselves or at least do business in the community.

The parents of students who hold lead roles in the production should be asked to serve on the parent promotional committee. Potential patrons should be approached at the beginning of the theatre season or during the first production. Give a press release to the local newspapers, naming the present promotional committee and letting the community know that they will be selling ads (see Figure 11.9).

In order not to exclude prospective patrons, an advertisement can run in the local newspaper. This will cover the entire community so that no one will feel left out if he or she is not contacted personally. Such an advertisement will almost always generate additional patrons (see Figure 11.10).

Also, send a letter to the school's faculty and staff, and include the entire district personnel. Support from the junior high and elementary schools is vital to the success of your program (see Figure 11.11).

After you have a committee, have set prices, and have compiled a list of prospective patrons, it is necessary to designate a Parent Promotional Committee Chairperson. This person, or couple, will save you much time. Committee members will report to the chairperson, who will keep records and maintain a consistent watch over the committee to see that the ads are being collected. To help with this process, supply the committee with collection envelopes, patron forms, and informative fliers. To ensure clear, accurate records, a patron record sheet should be attached to each envelope. This allows each committee member to keep a record of his or her patrons and allows the chairperson to easily tally each collected envelope (see Figure 11.12).

PAYMENT PROCEDURE

The patrons should be encouraged to pay by check, which then becomes their receipt for tax purposes. If some patrons do pay in cash, you may need to forward them a receipt for their records. It may be a good idea to check with your school's bookkeeper to find out the procedure for handling funds at your school.

Many times it is necessary to send a statement requesting payment for the ad. This can be done very quickly by printing a statement form and filling in the necessary information (see Figure 11.13).

WINDOW CARD

After a patron has paid for the ad, he or she should be given a window card to display, advertising his or her patronage of your theatre department. This is great public relations for the entire year, as it is a lasting reminder of community support. The card should be approximately 4 × 8 inches and should include artwork and printed in school colors to make it more attractive (see Figure 11.14).

PATRON COVER LETTER

Once your patrons' money is collected, send the patrons the information needed to secure their tickets to the productions. Include a cover letter, a season flier or individual show flier, a ticket order form, and patron coupons. (An explanation of the season and individual show flier can be found in Chapter 1. A discussion and examples of the ticket order form may be found in Chapter 9.)

The purpose of the patron cover letter is to explain clearly how to use the patron coupons. Also included in the letter should be ticket information and a general thank you for the financial support of the patron. An attempt should be made to tie in the theatre season theme and include any other information that will make the process of securing tickets and attending the show easier (see Figure 11.15).

PATRON COUPONS

Patron coupons can be made very easily. Some schools distribute actual tickets to their patrons, but this is not a good idea since you have no guarantee that the tickets are going to be used. The patron coupon takes care of this problem.

Make sure it is clear that the coupon is not a ticket and that the coupon must be exchanged in advance of the show. If the patron is in need of additional tickets, he or she may then order them by using the ticket form you enclose (see Figures 11.16 and 11.17).

By adding patrons to the program, your department can become self-supporting. Many directors must support their productions by selling or by having bake sales, car washes, and so on. However, I believe, as a theatre director, your time must be spent directing and teaching, not fund raising. The financial support of patrons will allow you to put your effort into the production along with building a strong foundation for your department.

FIGURE 11.1   Display ads.

PATRONS OF THE FINE ARTS

Mr. & Mrs. Ronald Ray
G. William Gray
Mr. & Mrs. Carl Smart
The Ned Bixler Family
Mr. & Mrs. Dennis Gable
Bill & Karyl Summers & Family
Mr. & Mrs. Randall Polter
CHS Kitchen Staff—Dorothy, Joyce, Nina, Rosie, Jonie, Anna Rose, Betty
Mr. & Mrs. Roland Baker
Miss Nancy Hanger
Mr. & Mrs. James B. Carothers
Mr. & Mrs. James C. Carothers
Dianne Schoenfeld
Mr. & Mrs. Dan Schoenfeld
Mr. & Mrs. George Huston
Mrs. Evelyn Opelt
Mr. & Mrs. William Jones
Mrs. C.L. Woleslagel
Mr. & Mrs. John Golembiowski
John & Shar Murphy
Mr. & Mrs. James Avery
Luella M. Jackson
Mr. & Mrs. Ted Geiger
Miss Deborah Ryan
Mr. & Mrs. Philip A. Widman
Shirley A. Brown
Mr. & Mrs. George Buck
Kuns Drive In
Mr. & Mrs. Cliff Rogers
Ginny & Ken McKenzie
Mr. & Mrs. Richard Rader
Cindi Slotto
Mr. & Mrs. C.H. Wolfe
Orville & Mildred Carroll
Lisa Carroll
Mr. & Mrs. Tim Benincasa
Dr. & Mrs. J.F. Pascua
Mr. & Mrs. Daniel J. Burkett & Son
L & K Restaurant, Janice Smith, Mgr.
Dana L. Ritter
Mr. & Mrs. Howard L. Ritter
Ms. Kathy Ball
Mr. & Mrs. Robert Spicer

FIGURE 11.2   Name listings.

PATRONS

"An Evening with the GEHS Speech and Drama Department" is made possible by the financial contributions of the patrons listed below. We are privileged to have these friends sustaining our efforts. We invite you to become a patron for our future shows, and, as always, we thank all our patrons below.

SPECIAL ANGELS

Mr. & Mrs. Bill Bond, Gardner
Don Allenbrand, Dales Body Shop, Olathe
Executive Beechcraft, Inc., Industrial Airport
Sadler Liquor, Gardner
North Supply Company, Industrial Airport

ANGELS

Allenbrand-Drews & Associates, Olathe
Steve and Sherry Attig, Olathe
Ron and Sharon Beets, Gardner
Blazer Burger, Gardner
Clayton's Accounting, Gardner
Construction Materials, Inc., Gardner
Continental Telephone Co. of Kansas, Gardner
The Corner, Mr. and Mrs. Bill Mounkes, Gardner
Cramer Products, Inc., Gardner
Dazey Products Co., Industrial Airport
Emberton's Room, Gardner
The Elliott McCreary Insurance Inc., Olathe
Farmer's Bank and Trust, Gardner
Gardner Auto Supply, Inc., Gardner
Gardner Shortstop, Gardner
Gardner Tractor Co., Gardner
Mr. and Mrs. Gene Gay, Gardner
Mr. and Mrs. David C. Grinnell, Gardner
Hoch's Dari Freez, Carol and Tony Hoch, Gardner
Eileen and Renae Kurtz, Gardner
A. T. Reece, Gardner
Ella T. Reece, Gardner
Bill Richey, Shawnee
Harvey and Esther Seim, Gardner
Larry Sheldon, Olathe
Glenn and Betty Smith, Gardner
Stricker's Auction, Gardner
Dr. and Mrs. Whitaker, Gardner

(continued)

FIGURE 11.3   Name listings.

DONORS
Kim Beets, Gardner
City of Gardner, Kansas
John and Marlene Cochran, Gardner
Mike O'Connor, Gardner
Dee's Mini-Mart, Edgerton
Gardner Glass, Gardner
John and Martha Hodges, Gardner
Pioneer, Gardner
Stricker's Auction Co., Gardner
Dr. and Mrs. R. K. Thomen, Gardner
T-Shirts by Jean, Gardner

FIGURE 11.3   Continued.

FIGURE 11.4 Business cards.

INDIAN TRAIL JUNIOR HIGH

Presents

"The Butler Did It"

by Tim Kelly

Student Director ....Barry Hughes

Assistant ....Tiffany Coughlin

Stage Manager....................Lynn Thorp

Sponsor/Director .... Terry Simmons

House Manager ....Tammy Evans

There will be a 15 minute intermission between each act.

Produced by special arrangement with Baker's Plays of Boston.

FIGURE 11.5   Business cards.

GARDNER EDGERTON HIGH SCHOOL
THEATRE PROGRAM
1990 - 1991

_____ Yes, I would like to be included in the 1990 - 1991 Gardner Edgerton High School Theatre programs as a:

_____ Special Angel $100   (Will receive name in program, and four tickets to each show along with your name on a Special Angels board in the lobby of the auditorium)

_____ Angel $75   (Will receive name in program, and three tickets to each show)

_____ Donor $50   (Will receive name in program, and two tickets to each show)

_____ Sponsor $25   (Will receive name in program, and one ticket to each show)

_____ Check enclosed

_____ Cash enclosed

_____ Will send to the school: Theatre Programs
Gardner Edgerton High School
318 E. Washington Street
Gardner, Kansas 66030

Please fill out the following information as it will appear in the program:

Name of Firm _____

Address _____

City _____   Phone _____

• •

Examples:
SPECIAL ANGEL
Mr. and Mrs. J.B. Jones, Gardner
The National Bank and Savings Co., Olathe

ANGEL
West Baking Company, Gardner
Dr. and Mrs. James B. Heckelman, Edgerton

_____
AD SOLD AND COLLECTED BY

FIGURE 11.6   Display ad form.

Program Advertisement
Clyde High School's

BYE BYE BIRDIE

Name of Firm _____

Address _____

City _____ State _____ Zip Code _____

A page of the program measures 5 1/2 x 8 1/2

Check the size you want:

_____ 1/8 of page	$22.00
_____ 1/4 of page	$28.00
_____ 1/3 of page	$32.00
_____ 1/2 of page	$42.00
_____ FULL Page	$70.00
_____ Patron Contribution	_____

(Patrons are listed separately on a patron's page.)

WRITE YOUR AD BELOW:

Please return as soon as possible, but not later than February 27, 1991 to **BYE BYE BIRDIE** Program, Clyde High School, 1015 Race Street, Clyde, Ohio 43410.

FIGURE 11.7   Name listing form.

GEHS THEATRE PATRON FEATURES

1. FREE TICKETS
   Special Angels—four FREE tickets*
   Angels—three FREE tickets*
   Donors—two FREE tickets*
   Sponsors—one FREE ticket*
2. TAX DEDUCTIBLE
3. PRIORITY MAILINGS
4. NAME IN OVER 2500 PROGRAMS
5. NAME ON SPECIAL BOARD IN LOBBY OF THEATRE (Special Angels only)

JOIN YOUR NEIGHBORS AND FRIENDS IN SUPPORTING
GARDNER EDGERTON HIGH SCHOOL'S ANNIVERSARY SEASON OF THEATRE

*The number of free tickets is for each production, the performance of patron's choice.

FIGURE 11.8   Patron features.

Ticket Sales for Gardner Edgerton High School's musical comedy, "Damn Yankees," continues to be "on schedule" according to James R. Opelt, GEHS director of theatre. According to Opelt, tickets for both the musical and pre-dinner show have been selling great. Opelt encourages district patrons to purchase their tickets this week as good seats are going fast. Recent musicals and dinners at the school have been sellouts.

Opelt also said he appreciates the cooperation and continued support of Contel, which again is underwriting the cost of printing posters for the musical; the Farmers Bank and Trust Company for underwriting the cost of printing the tickets; and Design One, which is donating its time in executing the hair designs for the 1950s musical.

A special thanks is due the many patrons in the district who each year contribute over $3,000 to support the GEHS theatre department productions. Thanks also to the Parents' Promotional Committee of Dean and Janet Shaw (chairpersons), Billie and Cathy Biggs, Cheryl Bohrn, Tom and Donna Corwin, Ronald and Iris Franks, Cliffort and Cherry Hunt, Macalene Murphy, Ron and Donnie Piel, Wayne and Alice Follf, Harold and Marilyn Wolf, Tom and Chris Saner, Don and Debbie Woodley, Delbert and Louise Sawyer, and Glenn and Betty Smith.

Anyone wishing to become a patron in this season's theatre programs and who was not contacted may call the school for more information.

Tickets for the musical and pre-show dinner will continue to be on sale and can be purchased by calling or visiting the high school library at 884-7101, ext. 248.

FIGURE 11.9   Press release.

178

PATRONS OF THE FINE ARTS

As an individual interested in the Fine Arts, I would like to be included on the Patron's Page in the program of Clyde Senior High School's production of *"BYE BYE BIRDIE"*. The show is to be presented March 26, 27 and 28. Enclosed is my donation of $ _____.

_____
Signature of Donor
(as you would like your name to appear in the program)

Make checks payable to
CLYDE SENIOR HIGH SCHOOL THEATRE PRODUCTIONS
and mail to
Mrs. Ruth Ritter, charman, Parents' Promotional Committee for
"BYE BYE BIRDIE"
117 West Cherry, Clyde, Ohio 43410

Donations must be postmarked by February 27, 1991

FIGURE 11.10   Patron advertisement.

DEPARTMENT OF SPEECH AND THEATRE

GARDNER EDGERTON HIGH SCHOOL
318 EAST WASHINGTON
GARDNER, KANSAS 66030

James R. Opelt
Instructor & Director
913-884-7101

" The Home of The Trailblazers"

October 4

Dear Staff Member,

This year's fall musical "Bye Bye Birdie" will be presented by Gardner Edgerton High School on November 10th, 11th, and 12th. We're all very excited about this event and hope you can attend. However, the undertaking of such a production as this is a great financial one, and we are asking for your help.

We are contacting all business and professional people in our school district to become patrons in our three theatre programs (Bye Bye Birdie Program, the program for the January show, and the program for the April show).

There are four types of patrons. 1. Special Angel (donation of $75) 2. Angel (donation of $40) 3. Donor (donation of $30) 4. Sponsor (donation of $20). Names of all contributors will be printed in the programs of each of the three shows this year. As a special thanks to those who become special angel patrons, you will receive coupons redeemable for *two* free tickets to each of the three productions this year (a total of *6* free tickets); plus, your name will appear on a special patron board in the lobby of the theatre. Angel patrons will receive *one* free ticket to each of the three productions this year (a total of *3* free tickets).

Your contribution is tax deductible. Please pay by check if possible. If you would like to help us out with your contribution, please fill out the attached form and clip to it your check. Make checks payable to: Gardner-Edgerton High School.

Please return your completed form and check to me via inner school mail by Monday, October 10.

Sincerely,

James R. Opelt
Director of Theatre

lb:JO

"Dedicated to the Best in Educational Speech and Theatre"
UNIFIED SCHOOL DISTRICT NO. 231

FIGURE 11.11 School faculty letter.

"DAMN YANKEES"
1986 - 87 Program Patrons

Solictor _____   Please complete by _____

NAME	CITY	AD SIZE	MONEY ENCLOSED

Total Patrons _____   Total Money _____

FIGURE 11.12   Envelope tally sheet.

DEPARTMENT OF SPEECH AND THEATRE

GARDNER EDGERTON HIGH SCHOOL

318 EAST WASHINGTON
GARDNER, KANSAS 66030

James R. Opelt
Instructor & Director
913-884-7101

"The Home of The Trailblazers"

Dear Patrons,

    Our records indicate that you are a _____ in our theatre program. For this spot in our program would you please remit _____ to "Once Upon A Mattress," Gardner Edgerton High School, 318 E. Washington St., Gardner, Kansas 66030.

    As soon as we receive your remittance we will forward you your ticket coupons. If you have sent your payment, please disregard this reminder.

    Thank you for your time and support of our program.

                    Sincerely,

                    James R. Opelt
                    Director of Theatre

"Dedicated to the Best in Educational Speech and Theatre"
UNIFIED SCHOOL DISTRICT NO. 231

FIGURE 11.13 Statement form.

We Support and
Encourage Your Attendance

at

Gardner Edgerton
High School's
Theatre Productions.

199___ – 199___

FIGURE 11.14 Window card.

DEPARTMENT OF SPEECH AND THEATRE

GARDNER EDGERTON HIGH SCHOOL

318 EAST WASHINGTON
GARDNER, KANSAS 66030

James R. Opelt
Instructor & Director
913-884-7101

"The Home of The Trailblazers"

Dear Special Angels, Angels, Donors, and Sponsors,

It is with much appreciation that I welcome you as a patron of the Gardner Edgerton High School "Award Winning Season of Theatre." The three productions we have planned this year promise to be the area's best offering of educational theatre.

As you well know, our first production, the Tony award winning musical comedy, "Damn Yankees," is quickly approaching. Production dates are November 13, 14, and 15. Please find enclosed "patron coupons" to be redeemed for your free tickets(s).

I suggest that you select the performance you will attend and return your coupons immediately. We will then forward you your tickets. Remember, the enclosed coupon is not a ticket. You must exchange the coupon in advance of the show. If you are in need of more tickets, a ticket order form has been enclosed. Simply complete it and return it with your coupon(s) and a check for the additional amount.

I hope you will also encourage your friends to attend our productions. If you know someone who would like to be included in our mailings, please enclose their name and address with your ticket order.

Your financial support and attendance at our shows is vitally important to the success of our program. Thank you for your continued support.

Sincerely,

James R. Opelt
Director of Theatre

P.S. We will again be serving dinner before the Friday and Saturday performances of "Damn Yankees." I have enclosed a ticket order form if you are interested in joining us for dinner. Tickets for the dinner are limited, so return your request today.

Enclosures

"Dedicated to the Best in Educational Speech and Theatre"
UNIFIED SCHOOL DISTRICT NO. 231

FIGURE 11.15   Patron cover letter.

PATRON FREE TICKET COUPON

\# _____   _____ 1986

TO: _____

Redeemable for one student or one adult ticket to any performance of Gardner Edgerton High School's production of DAMN YANKEES, November 13, 14, and 15. It is suggested that this coupon be redeemed in advance of the show to assure good seating.

_____   _____
Director of Theatre   Not redeemable unless signed
                                 by patron named above

- -

PATRON FREE TICKET COUPON

\# _____   _____ 1986

TO: _____

Redeemable for one student or one adult ticket to any performance of Gardner Edgerton High School's production of DAMN YANKEES, November 13, 14, and 15. It is suggested that this coupon be redeemed in advance of the show to assure good seating.

_____   _____
Director of Theatre   Not redeemable unless signed
                                 by patron named above

- -

PATRON FREE TICKET COUPON

\# _____   _____ 1986

TO: _____

Redeemable for one student or one adult ticket to any performance of Gardner Edgerton High School's production of DAMN YANKEES, November 13, 14, and 15. It is suggested that this coupon be redeemed in advance of the show to assure good seating.

_____   _____
Director of Theatre   Not redeemable unless signed
                                 by patron named above

FIGURE 11.16   Patron coupon.

OLATHE SOUTH HIGH SCHOOL THEATRE

SHARE IT!

NOVEMBER 19–21
8:00 p.m.

Carousel
Music by RICHARD RODGERS
Book and Lyrics by OSCAR HAMMERSTEIN II

DECEMBER 12
1:30 & 8:00 p.m.

We the People

FEBRUARY 26 & 27
8:00 p.m.

Flowers for Algernon

MAY 6 & 7
8:00 p.m.

GEORGE WASHINGTON SLEPT HERE

FIGURE 11.17   Patron coupon (front). (Courtesy of Stan Adell)

FREE TICKET COUPON

OLATHE SOUTH HIGH SCHOOL THEATRE

SHARE IT!

1987 - 88 SEASON

\# _____

TO:

Redeemable for one student or one adult ticket to any performance of the Olathe South High School production indicated below. It is suggested that this coupon be redeemed in advance of the show to assure good seating. This coupon is not a ticket.

Director of Theatre

Not redeemable unless signed by person named above

☐ **CAROUSEL**
NOVEMBER 19-21

☐ **WE THE PEOPLE**
DECEMBER 12

☐ **FLOWERS FOR ALGERNON**
FEBRUARY 26 & 27

☐ **GEORGE WASHINGTON SLEPT HERE**
MAY 6 & 7

FIGURE 11.18 Patron coupon (back). (Courtesy of Stan Adell)

12

Suggested Plays for Production and Study

The following list of plays has been compiled by Barry Alexander. The type of play is indicated by (C) for comedy and (D) for drama. The author's name and publisher is given. The possibility of monologues, scenes, and play excerpts (for one-act festivals) for each show has been noted. The (M) indicates Male, (F) Female, and (L) possibly objectionable language. The publishers are designated as Dramatic Play Service (DPS), Samuel French (SF), and Dramatic Publishing Company (DPC). I have also indicated (X) those shows which, in my opinion, lend themselves to high school productions. Remember: Each school and community will differ in what may or may not be acceptable; therefore, all scripts should be read thoroughly before deciding on a show or scene for presentation. No shows or scenes should ever be performed without securing permission from the publisher and paying all necessary royalties.

Play/Type	Author	Monologues	Scenes	Play Excerpts	Publisher	High School
The Actor's Nightmare (C)	Christopher Durang	M (L)			DPS	
After the Fall (D)	Arther Miller	MF	MF		DPS	
Agnes of God (D)	John Pielmeier	F	F	F	SF	
Ah Wilderness (C)	Eugene O'Neill		MF		SF	X
Album (C)	David Rimmer		MF	MF	DPS	
All My Sons (D)	Arthur Miller	M	MF	MF	DPS	X
All the Way Home (D)	Tad Mosel		MF		SF	
Alone Together (C)	Lawrence Roman	F	MF	MF	SF	
Amadeus (D)	Peter Shaffer	M	MF		SF	X
American Buffalo (D)	David Mamet		M (L)	M (L)	SF	
Anastasia (D)	Guy Bolton	F	F	F	SF	
And a Nightingale Sang (D)	C. P. Taylor		MF	MF	DPC	
And Miss Reardon Drinks a Little (C)	Paul Zindel		F	F	DPS	X
Angel Street (D)	Patrick Hamilton	MF	MF	MF	SF	X
Anne of the Thousand Days (D)	Marwell Anderson	MF	MF	MF	DPS	X
Antigone (D)	Lewis Galantier	MF	MF	MF	SF	
Any Wednesday (C)	Muriel Resnick		MF	MF	DPS	
Arms and the Man (C)	George Bernard Shaw		MF	MF	SF	
As Is (DC)	William M. Hoffman	M (L)	M (L)		DPS	
Ask Any Girl	Winifred Wolfe		MF	MF	DPC	
Aunt Dan and Lemon (C)	Wallace Shawn		MF		DPS	
The Autumn Garden (D)	Lillian Hellman	F	F	F	DPS	
The Bad Seed (D)	Maxwell Anderson		F	F	DPS	X
Barefoot in the Park (C)	Neil Simon		MF	MF	SF	X
Barretts of Wimpole Street (D)	Rudolf Besier		MF	MF	DPS	X
Becket (D)	Jean Anouilh	M	M		SF	X
Belle of Amherst (D)	William Luce	F			SF	X
Benefactors (C)	Michael Frayn		MF		SF	
Bent (D)	Martin Sherman		M (L)		SF	
Betrayal (D)	Harold Pinter		MF		DPS	
Beyond the Horizon (D)	Eugene O'Neill		MF		DPS	
Beyond Therapy (C)	Christopher Durang		MF		SF	
Biloxi Blues (C)	Neil Simon		MF		SF	X
Blithe Spirit (C)	Noel Coward		MF		SF	X
Blue Denium (D)	James Leo Herlihy		MF		SF	

190

Born Yesterday (C)	Garson Kanin		MF	MF	DPS	X
Bosoms and Neglect (C)	John Guare		MF	MF	DPS	
The Boys in Autumn (C)	Mernard Sabath		M	M	DPC	
Boys in the Band (DC)	Mart Crowley	M (L)	M (L)		SF	X
Brighton Beach Memoirs (DC)	Neil Simon	MF	MF		SF	X
Broadway Bound (C)	Neil Simon	MF	MF		SF	
Butley (DC)	Simon Gray		MF (L)		SF	
Butterflies Are Free (C)	Leonard Gershe	MF	MF	MF	SF	X
Cactus Flower (C)	Abe Burrows		MF		SF	X
California Suite (C)	Neil Simon	M	MF	MF	SF	X
Caligula (D)	Albert Camus	MF	MF		SF	
Candida (C)	George Bernard Shaw		MF		SF	
Career (D)	James Lee		MF		SF	
Cat On a Hot Tin Roof (D)	Tennessee Williams	MF	MF	MF	DPS	X
The Chalk Garden (D)	Enid Bagnold		F	F	SF	
Chapter Two (C)	Neil Simon	MF	MF	MF	SF	X
Children of a Lesser God (D)	Mark Medoff	M	MF	MF	DPS	X
The Children's Hour (D)	Lillian Hellman	F	MF		DPS	X
Child's Play (D)	Robert Marasco	M	M		SF	X
Clair De Lune (C)	Romulus Linney		MF	MF	DPS	
Clarence Darrow (D)	David W. Rintels	M			SF	
A Clearing in the Woods (DC)	Arthur Laurents	F	MF		DPS	
Close Ties (D)	Elizabeth Diggs		MF		DPS	
Cloud 9 (C)	Caryl Churchill	MF (L)	MF (L)	MF (L)	SF	
Coastal Disturbances (C)	Tina Howe		MF	MF	SF	
Come Back, Little Sheba (D)	William Inge		MF		SF	
Come Blow Your Horn (C)	Neil Simon		MF		SF	
The Common Pursuit (DC)	Simon Gray		MF		DPS	
Compulsion (D)	Meyer Evin	M	M		DPS	
The Corn is Green (D)	Emlyn Williams		MF		DPS	
Coupla White Chicks Sitting Around Talking (C)	John Ford Noonan	F	F	F	SF	
Court Martial of Billy Budd (D)	James M. Salem		M	M	DPC	
Crimes of the Heart (DC)	Beth Henley	M	MF		DPS	
Cyrano de Bergerac (C)	Edmond Rostand	M	MF		DPS	
Da (C)	Hugh Leonard	M	M		SF	
Dark at the Top of the Stairs (D)	William Inge	MF	MF		DPS	X
Dark Victory (D)	George Brewer, Jr.		MF		DPS	

(continued)

191

Play/Type	Author	Monologues	Scenes	Play Excerpts	Publisher	High School
David and Lisa (D)	James Reach		MF		SF	
The Day After the Fair (D)	Frank Harvey		MF		SF	
The Days Between (D)	Robert Anderson		MF		SF	
Days of Wine and Roses (D)	J. P. Miller		MF		DPS	
Death of a Salesman (D)	Arthur Miller	MF	MF		DPS	X
Deathtrap (D)	Ira Levin	M	M		DPS	X
A Delicate Balance (D)	Edward Albee	MF	MF		SF	
Desire Under the Elms (D)	Eugene O'Neill	MF	MF		DPS	
Detective Story (D)	Ira Levin	M	M		DPS	
Dial "M" for Murder (D)	Frederick Knott		MF		DPS	X
Diary of Adam and Eve (C)	Marc Bucci	MF	MF	MF	DPC	
The Diary of Anne Frank (D)	Frances Goodrich/ Albert Hackett	F	MF		DPS	X
The Dining Room (DC)	A. R. Guerney, Jr.		MF	MF	DPS	X
Dino (D)	Reginald Rese	M	MF		DPC	
The Diviners (D)	James Leonard		MF		SF	
A Doll's House (D)	Henrik Ibsen	F	MF		DPS	X
Don't Drink the Water (C)	Woody Allen		MF		SF	X
The Dresser (D)	Ronald Harwood	M	M		SF	
Driving Miss Daisy (D)	Alfred Uhry		MF		DPS	X
Duel of Angels (C)	Jean Giraudoux		F		DPS	
Duet for One (D)	Tom Kempinski	F	MF		SF	
Edward, My Son (D)	Robert Morley/ Noel Langley		MF		DPS	
The Effect of Gamma Rays On Man-in-the-Moon Marigolds (D)	Paul Zindel	F	F	F	DPS	X
The Elephant Man (D)	Bernard Pomerance	M	MF		DPS	
Elizabeth the Queen (D)	Maxwell Anderson	MF	MF		DPS	X
The Entertainer (C)	John Osborne	M			DPC	
Equus (D)	Peter Shaffer	MF	MF		DPS	
Everything in the Garden (C)	Edward Albee		MF (L)		DPS	
Execution of Justice (D)	Emily Mann	M (L)	MF (L)		DPS	
Extremities (D)	William Mastrosimone		MF (L)		DPS	
Father's Day (C)	Oliver Hailey	F	F (3)		DPS	
Flowers For Algernon (D)	David Rogers	M	MF		DPC	X

Fool For Love (C)	Sam Shepard				DPS	X
Fools (C)	Neil Simon	M	MF (L)		SF	X
Fortune and Men's Eyes (D)	John Herbert		M (L)		SF	
Forty Carats (C)	Jay Allen		MF	MF	SF	
The Fourposter (C)	Jan de Hartog		MF		SF	
Foxfire (D)	Susan Cooper/ Hume Cronyn	MF	MF	MF	SF	
Galileo (D)	Bertold Brecht	M	M		SF	
Gemini (C)	Albert Innaurato	M	MF		DPS	
The Gin Game (C)	D. L. Coburn		MF		SF	
The Gingerbread Lady (DC)	Neil Simon	MF	MF	MF	SF	X
The Glass Menagerie (D)	Tennessee Williams	MF	MF	MF	DPS	
Glengarry Glen Ross (D)	David Mamet		M (L)	M (L)	SF	
God's Favorite (C)	Neil Simon		M		SF	
The Good Doctor (C)	Neil Simon	MF	MF	MF	SF	X
Goodbye Charlie (C)	George Axelrod		MF		SF	X
Greater Tuna (C)	Jaston Williams		M	M	SF	X
The Grass Harp (C)	Truman Capote		MF		SF	X
Hadrian the Seventh (DC)	Peter Luck		M		DPS	
Harold and Maude (C)	Colin Higgins	MF	MF		SF	
Harvey (C)	Mary Chase	M	MF		SF	
The Hasty Heart (D)	John Patrick		MF		DPS	X
A Hatful of Rain (D)	Michael V. Gasso		MF		DPS	X
Hay Fever (C)	Noel Coward		MF		SF	
Heaven Can Wait (C)	Harry Segall		MF		SF	
Hedda Gabler (D)	Henrik Ibsen		AMF		DPS	
The Heiress (D)	Ruth & Augustus Goetz		MF	MF	DPS	X
Home of the Brave (D)	Arthur Laurents		M	M (3+)	DPS	
The Homecoming (D)	Harold Pinter		MF		SF	
The Hot L Baltimore (C)	Lanford Wilson	F	M	F	DPS	
The House of Bernarda Alba (D)	Frederico Garcia Lorca	F	F		SF	
How I Got That Story (C)	Amlin Gray	M	M	M	DPS	
Hughie (C)	Eugene O'Neill	M	M		DPS	
Hurlyburly (D)	David Rabe		MF (L)		SF	
I Am a Camera (C)	John Van Druten	MF (L)	MF		DPS	
I Never Sang For My Father (D)	Robert Anderson	M	MF		DPS	X
I Remember Mama (D)	John Van Druten	F	MF	MF	DPS	X

(continued)

193

Play/Type	Author	Monologues	Scenes	Play Excerpts	Publisher	High School
I'm Getting My Act Together and Taking It On the Road (C)	Gretchen Cryer	F	FM	FM	SF	
The Importance of Being Earnest (C)	Oscar Wilde		MF	MF (2+)	SF	X
The Impossible Years (C)	Bob Fisher	M	MF		SF	
In Praise of Love (C)	Terence Rattigan		MF		SF	
Incident at Vichy (D)	Arthur Miller	M	M (2+)		DPS	
Inherit the Wind (D)	Jerome Lawrence/ Robert E. Lee	M	MF	DPS	DPS	X
Invitation to a March (C)	Arthur Laurents	F	FM		DPS	
Is There Life After High School? (C)	Jeffrey Kindley	MF			SF	
Isn't It Romantic (C)	Wendy Wasserstein		MF		DPS	
It Had to Be You (C)	Renee Taylor/ Joseph Bologna		MF	MF	SF	
Jenny Kissed Me (C)	Jean Kerr		MF		DPS	
Jimmy Shine (C)	Murray Shisgal	M	MF		DPS	
Joan of Lorraine (D)	Maxwell Anderson	F	FM		DPS	
Johnny Belinda (D)	Elmer Harris		MF		DPS	
K2 (D)	Patrick Meyers		M	M	DPS	
Kennedy's Children (D)	Robert Patrick	MF	MF	MF (6)	SF	X
Key Exchange (C)	Kevin Wade	M (L)	MF (L)	MF (L)	DPS	
Lady From Dubuque (D)	Edward Albee	F	MF		DPS	
Ladyhouse Blues (D)	Kevin O'Morrison	F	F		SF	
The Last of Mrs. Lincoln (D)	James Prideaux	F	MF		DPS	
Les Liaisons Dangereuses (D)	Christopher Hampton		MF		SF	X
The Lesson (C)	Eugene Tonesco		MF	MF (3)	SF	
A Lie of the Mind (D)	Sam Shepard	MF (L)	M	M	DPS	
A Life in the Theatre (D)	David Mamet		MF	M (3)	SF	
Life With Father (C)	Howard Lindsay/ Russel Crouse		MF		DPS	X
Liliom (D)	Fereno Molnar		MF		SF	
Lion in Winter (D)	James Goldman		MF		SF	X
The Little Foxes (D)	Lillian Hellman	F	MF		DPS	
Long Day's Journey Into Night (D)	Eugene O'Neill	MF	MF		DPS	X
Look Back in Anger (D)	John Osborne	M	MF		DPC	X
Look Homeward, Angel (D)	Ketti Frings	M	MF		SF	X

Loose Ends (D)	Michael Weller		MF		SF	
A Loss of Roses (D)	William Inge	F	MF		DPS	
Lovers and Other Strangers (C)	Renee Taylor/ Joseph Bologna		MF	MF	SF	
Lunch Hour (C)	Jean Kerr		MF		SF	
Luther (D)	John Osborne	M	M		DPC	
Luv (C)	Murray Schisgal	M	MF		DPS	
The Madwoman of Chaillot (C)	Jean Giraudoux	MF	F		DPS	
Magic Time (C)	James Sherman	M	MF		SF	
Major Barbara (C)	George Bernard Shaw	MF	MF		SF	
Man and Superman (C)	George Bernard Shaw	MF	MF		SF	X
A Man Called Peter (D)	Catherine Marshall	M	MF	MF (4)	DPC	X
A Man for All Seasons (D)	Robert Bolt	M	MF		SF	X
Marat/Sade (D)	Peter Weiss	MF	MF		DPC	
The Marriage of Bette and Boo (C)	Christopher Durang	F	MF		DPS	
The Marriage Go-round (C)	Leslie Stevens	MF	MF		SF	
Mary of Scotland (D)	Maxwell Anderson	F	F	MF (3)	SF	
Mass Appeal (DC)	Bill C. Davis	M	M	M	DPS	
The Matchmaker (C)	Thornton Wilder	MF	MF		SF	X
Medea (D)	Robinson Jeffers	MF	MF		SF	X
Middle of the Night (D)	Paddy Chayefsky	M	M		SF	
The Miracle Worker (D)	William Gibson	F	F		SF	
The Misanthrope (C)	Moliere	M	MF		SF	X
The Miser (C)	Moliere (Miles Mallison)	MF	MF		SF	
The Miss Firecracker Contest (C)	Beth Henley	F	F		DPS	
Miss Julie (D)	August Strindberg (Harry Carlson)	F	MF	MF	SF	
Miss Margarida's Way (C)	Roberto Athayde	F	FM		SF	
Monday After the Miracle (D)	William Gibson	F	F	F (1)	DPS	
Monique (D)	Dorothy/Michael Blankfort		F		SF	X
A Moon for the Misbegotten (D)	Eugene O'Neill	MF	MF		SF	
The Moon is Blue (C)	F. Hugh Herbert	MF	MF		DPS	
More Stately Mansions (D)	Eugene O'Neill		MF		DPC	
Mourning Becomes Electra (D)	Eugene O'Neill		MF		DPS	
My Cousin Rachel (D)	Diana Morgan		MF		DPS	
My Fat Friend (C)	Charles Laurence		MF		SF	

(continued)

Play/Type	Author	Monologues	Scenes	Play Excerpts	Publisher	High School
My Sister Eileen (C)	Joseph Fields/ Jerome Chodorov		F		DPS	X
My Three Angels (C)	Sam & Bella Spewack		MF		DPS	
Natural Affection (D)	William Inge		MF		DPS	
Ned and Jack (D)	Sheldon Rosen	M	M	M	SF	
The Nerd (C)	Larry Shue	M	MF		DPS	X
Never Too Late (C)	Sumner Arthur Long	M	MF		SF	
The Night of the Iguana (D)	Tennessee Williams	MF	MF		DPS	
'Night, Mother (D)	Marsha Norman	F	F	F	DPS	X
The Night Thoreau Spent in Jail (D)	Jerome Lawrence/ Robert E. Lee	M	MF		SF	X
Nightwatch (D)	Lucille Fletcher	F	MF		DPS	
Noel Coward in Two Keys (C)	Noel Coward		MF	MF (3)	SF	X
The Normal Heart (D)	Larry Kramer	M (L)	MF (L)		SF	
Nuts (D)	Tom Topor	F (L)	MF (L)		SF	
Odd Couple (C)	Neil Simon (both versions)		M and F		SF	X
Of Mice and Men (D)	John Steinbeck		M		DPS	X
Oh, Dad, Poor Dad, Mamma's Hung You in the Closet (C)	Arthur Kopit	FM	FM	FM (3 or 4) OR 4)	SF	X
On Borrowed Time (C)	Paul Osborn	M	MF		DPS	X
On Golden Pond (C)	Ernest Thompson		MF	MF (6)	DPS	X
One Flew Over the Cuckoo's Nest (C)	Dale Wasserman	M	MF		SF	X
Open Admissions (D)	Shirly Laure	MF	MF	MF	SF	
Ordinary People (D)	Judith Guest		MF		DPC	X
Orphans (C)	Lyle Kessler	M	M	M (3)	SF	
Our Town (D)	Thornton Wilder	MF	MF		SF	X
The Owl and the Pussycat (C)	Bill Manhoff		MF	MF	SF	
Pack of Lies (D)	Hugh Whitemore	M	MF		SF	
Period of Adjustment (C)	Tennessee Williams	F	MF		DPS	
The Philadelphia Story (C)	Phillip Barry		MF		SF	X
Picnic (D)	William Inge	M	MF		DPS	X
Pillow Talk (C)	Stanley Shapiro		MF		DPC	X
Plaza Suite (C)	Neil Simon	M	MF	MF	SF	X
The Pleasure of His Company (C)	Samuel Taylor		MF		DPS	X

196

Plenty (D)	David Hare	F	MF		SF	
Portrait of Jennie (D)	Robert Nathan		MF		DPC	
The Prime of Miss Jean Brodie (D)	Jay Allen	F	MF		SF	X
The Prisoner of Second Avenue (C)	Neil Simon	M	MF		SF	X
The Private Ear (C)	Peter Shaffer	M	MF	MF (3)	SF	X
Private Lies (C)	Noel Coward	M	MF	MF (3)	SF	X
The Promise (D)	Aleksei Arbusov		MF		DPS	
P.S. Your Cat is Dead! (C)	James Kirkwood		MF		SF	
Pygmalion	George Bernard Shaw	MF	MF		SF	X
The Rainmaker (D)	N. Richard Nash	M	MF		SF	X
A Raisin in the Sun (D)	Lorraine Hansberry	MF	MF		SF	X
The Real Thing (D)	Tom Stoppard	MF	MF		SF	
Rebel Without a Cause (D)	James Fuller		MF		DPC	X
The Reluctant Debutante (C)	William Douglas Home		MF		SF	
The Remarkable Mr. Pennypacker (C)	Liam O'Brien		MF		SF	
Rhinoceros (C)	Eugene Ionesco	M	MF		SF	
The Robe (D)	Lloyd C. Douglas		MF		DPC	X
Romantic Comedy (C)	Bernard Slade	MF	MF		SF	
A Roomful of Roses (DC)	Edith Sommer	F	MF		DPS	
The Rope Dancers (D)	Morton Wishengrad		MF		SF	
The Rose Tatoo (D)	Tennessee Williams		MF		S	
Rosencrantz and Guildenstern Are Dead (C)	Tom Stoppard		MF		SF	
The Royal Family (C)	George S. Kaufman/ Edna Ferber	F	MF		SF	
The Royal Hunt of the Sun (D)	Peter Shaffer	M	M		SF	
Runaways (D) (musical)	Elizabeth Swados	MF	MF		SF	
The Runner Stumbles (D)	Milan Stitt	MF	MF		DPS	
Sabrina Fair (C)	Samuel Tylor		MF		DPS	
Saint Joan (D)	George Bernard Shaw	MF	MF		SF	
Same Time, Next Year (C)	Bernard Slade		MF	MF	SF	
Say Goodnight, Gracie (C)	Ralph Pape	M	MF		DPS	
Scuba Duba (C)	Bruce Jay Friedman	M	MF		DPS	
The Sea Gull (D)	Anton Chekhov (Michael Frayn)	MF	MF		SF	
The Sea Horse (D)	Edward J. Moore		MF (L)		SF	
Sea Marks (D)	Gardner McKay		MF (L)		SF	
The Secret Affairs of Mildred Wild (C)	Paul Zindel	F	MF	MF	DPS	
Separate Tables (D)	Terence Rattigan		MF	MF	SF	

(continued)

197

Play/Type	Author	Monologues	Scenes	Play Excerpts	Publisher	High School
The Seven Year Itch (C)	George Axelrod	M	MF		DPS	
The Shadow Box (D)	Michael Cristoffer	MF (L)	MF (L)		SF	X
The Shrike (D)	Joseph Kramm		MF		DPS	
Silent Night, Lonely Night (D)	Robert Anderson		MF		SF	
Sister Mary Ignatius Explains It All For You (C)	Christopher Durang	F (L)			DPS	
Sleuth (D)	Anthony Shaffer	M	M	M	SF	
Slyfox (C)	Larry Gelbart	M	MF	MF	SF	
Social Security (C)	Andrew Bergman		MF		SF	
Solomon's Child (D)	Tom Dulack	M	MF	M	DPS	
Some Men Need Help (C)	John Ford Noonan		M	M	SF	
Sorrows and Sons (D)	Stephen Metcalfe	M	MF	MF	SF	
Splendor in the Grass (D)	F. Andrew Leslie	MF	MF		DPS	X
Spoon River Anthology (D)	Charles Aidman	M		MF	SF	X
Stage Struck (D)	Simon Gray	M	M		SF	
Stalag 17 (DC)	Donald Bevan/ Edmund Trzcinski		M (2+)		DPS	
Star Spangled Girl (C)	Neil Simon	MF	MF	F (6)	DPS	X
Steel Magnolias (C)	Robert Harling	F	F	MF (2+)	DPS	X
Story Theatre (C)	Paul Sills			F (6)	SF	X
Strange Interlude (D)	Eugene O'Neill	F	F	MF (3)	DPS	
Strange Snow (D)	Steve Metcalfe	MF	MF		SF	
Streamers (D)	David Rabe	M (L)	M (L)		SF	
A Streetcar Named Desire (D)	Tennessee Williams	F	MF		DPS	X
The Subject Was Roses (D)	Frank Gilroy	MF	MF	MF	SF	
Suddenly Last Summer (D)	Tennessee Williams	F	MF	MF	DPS	
Summer and Smoke (D)	Tennessee Williams	MF	MF		DPS	
Summertree (D)	Ron Cowen	MF	MF	MF	DPS	
Sunday in New York (C)	Norman Krasna		MF		DPS	
Sweet Bird of Youth (D)	Tennessee Williams	MF	MF	MF	DPS	
Sweet Sue (C)	A. R. Guerney, Jr.	F	MF		DPS	
Table Settings (C)	James Lapine	M	MF		SF	
Take Her, She's Mine (C)	Phoebe and Henry Ephron	M	MF		SF	
Talking With (D)	Jane Martin	F		F	SF	

Talley's Folly (C)	Landford Wilson	M	MF	MF	DPS	X
Tea and Sympathy (D)	Robert Anderson	MF	MF	MF	AF	X
Teach Me How to Cry (D)	Patricia Joudry		MF		DPS	
Tell Me That You Love Me, Junie Moon (D)	Marjorie Kellog	MF	MF		DPC	
The Tender Trap (C)	Max Shulman/ Robt. Paul Smith		MF		DPS	X
Terra Nova (D)	Ted Tally	MF	MF		DPS	
That Championship Season (D)	Jason Miller	M	M	M (5)	DPS	X
There's a Girl in My Soup (C)	Terence Frisby		MF		SF	X
A Thousand Clowns (C)	Herb Gardner	M	MF		SF	X
A Thurber Carnival (C)	James Thurber		MF	MF (5+)	SF	
The Time of Your Life (D)	William Saroyan	M	MF		SF	
Times Square (D)	Leonard Melfi	MF (L)	MF (L)		SF	
Tiny Alice (D)	Edward Albee	MF (L)	MF (L)		DPS	
To Kill a Mockingbird (D)	Christopher Sergal	MF	MF		DPC	
Top Girls (C)	Caryl Churchill	F	F	F (2+)	SF	
Torch Song Trilogy (C)	Harvey Feirstein		MF (L)	MF (L)	SF	X
Toys in the Attic (D)	Lillian Hellman	M (L)	MF		DPS	
Tracers (D)	John DiFusco	M	MF	M (5)	DPS	
Tribute (C)	Bernard Slade	M	M	M	SF	
True West (C)	Sam Shepard	M	MF	M	SF	
Twice Around the Park (C)	Murray Schisgal	M	MF	MF	SF	
Twigs (C)	George Furth	F	MF	MF	SF	
Two for the Seesaw (DC)	William Gibson	MF	MF	MF	SF	
University (D)	Jon Jory	MF	MF	MF	DPC	
The Unknown Soldier and His Wife (D)	Peter Ustinov	MF	MF		SF	
Up the Down Staircase (C)	Christopher Sergal		MF		DPC	
Vanities (C)	Jack Heifner		F (3)	F (3)	SF	
Veronica's Room (D)	Ira Levin		MF (3)		SF	X
A View From the Bridge	Arthur Miller	M	MF	M (1)	DPS	X
Vincent (D)	Leonard Nimoy	M	MF		DPC	
The Visit (D)	Friedrich Durrenmatt		MF		SF	
The Voice of the Turtle (C)	John van Druten		MF		DPS	
Voices From the High School (D)	Peter Dee		MF	MF	SF	
Wait Until Dark (D)	Frederick Knott		MF		DPS	
Waiting for the Parade (D)	John Murrell	F	F	F (5)	SF	
Watch on the Rhine (D)	Lillian Hellman	MF	MF		DPS	X
The West Side Waltz (C)	Ernest Thompson	F	F		DPS	

(continued)

Play/Type	Author	Monologues	Scenes	Play Excerpts	Publisher	High School
What I Did Last Summer (DC)	A. R. Gurney, Jr.		MF		DPS	
When You Comin' Back, Red Ryder (C)	Mark Medoff	M	MF		DPS	
Who's Afraid of Virginia Woolf? (C)	Edward Albee	M	MF (L)		DPS	
Whose Life Is It, Anyway (D)	(both male/female versions)	MF	MF		DPC	X
Wild Honey (C)	Michael Frayn	M	MF		SF	
Winesburg, Ohio (D)	Sherwood Anderson		MF		DPC	X
Wings (D)	Arthur Kopit	F	MF		SF	
The Wisdom of Eve (D)	Mary Orr/ Reginald Denham	MF	MF		DPS	
Woman in Mind (C)	Alan Ayckbourn	F	MF		SF	
Years Ago (DC)	Ruth Gordon		MF		SF	
Zelda	William Luce	F		F (1)	SF	
The Zoo Story (D)	Edward Albee	M	M	M	SF	X

13

Selecting a Musical

Selecting a musical for production is much more difficult than selecting a play because of the numerous elements involved in a musical. The story lines of musicals from the 1940s through 1970s are most suitable for high school performance and production. Musicals from these periods are of the "boy meets girl and everyone lives happily every after" theme. Many of the musicals that arrived on Broadway in the late 1970s and 1980s dealt with more mature topics. The Broadway musicals of the 80s, mostly English imports, also called for more elaborate sets and staging; for example, *Best Little Whorehouse in Texas* (1978), *Dreamgirls* (1981), *Cats* (1982), *Nine* (1982), *Les Miserables* (1987), *Starlight Express* (1987), *Phantom of the Opera* (1988), and *Aspects of Love* (1990). These shows and others like them are probably best left to be performed by professional theatres and touring companies.

Still, many critics long for the musical theatre to return to that "golden age." Theatre critic Ken Mandelbaum recently wrote in his review of the 1989 revival of *Gypsy* (1959), "I can only say that I found myself choked up on several occasions during the evening. This was the result of recalling the perfectionism and craftsmanship that was the Broadway musical of thirty years ago."

There are some theatres across the country that are dedicated to reviving old works and finding ones that come close to repeating that "golden age." One of the most notable is the Goodspeed Opera House in East Haddam, Connecticut. The Paper Mill Playhouse of Millburn, New Jersey, also presents new American works, and the College Conservatory of Music at the University of Cincinnati holds a Festival of New Works every year.

However, at present, we who work in secondary educational theatre may still be in the best position, for we choose our productions from that wonderful era of American musicals.

MUSICALS FOR PRODUCTION

Following is a list of 43 of the most performed musicals in secondary educational theatre. I have included the name of the leasing agent and whether the film version of the show is available on videocassette. By watching the film you can get ideas on costumes, sets, and choreography. Also, a list of the Original Cast Recording(s) is noted, as well as an indication if the show, as of this printing, is available on compact disk. Several shows have been recorded more than once with different casts. London recordings have also been listed. It should be noted that some original cast recordings, tapes, and videos are out of print and then re-released; check for availability. I have also included a short suggestion as to the performability of the shows.

Annie (Music Theatre International) (1982)

> (COL–34712, CD: CBS)
> Calls for several small girls but is an audience pleaser.

Annie Get Your Gun (Rodgers and Hammerstein Library) (1950)

> (RCA LOC–1124, Metro–548, DECCA DL–9018)
> A very popular show that needs a large cast and children.

Anything Goes (Tams-Witmark) (1936)

> (EPIC–13100/FLS–15100/DEC–8318/MCA–37092, CD: ANGEL-CAPITOL/EPIC EK–15100)
> A fun show with many good characters.

Bells Are Ringing (Tams-Witmark) (1960)

> (COL OL–5170/COL OS–2006, CD: COL-CBS CK 2006)
> This show may need some updating but is easy to direct.

The Boy Friend (Music Theatre International) (1971)

> (RCA LOC–1018, CD: RCA 60056–2–RG)
> Fun show with good music.

Brigadoon (Tams-Witmark) (1954, MGM/UA Home Video)

(COL CL-1132/RCA LOC-1001/MGM E-3135, CD: RCA)
A dramatic show that must have authentic costuming.

Bye Bye Birdie (Tams-Witmark) (1963, RCA/Columbia Pictures Home Video)

(COL-5510/COL OS-2025/RCA LOC-1081/RCA KOS-3040, CD: COL-CBS CK-2025)
Because of its 1950s theme it is very popular with students. An easy first musical.

Camelot (Tams-Witmark) (1967)

(COL KOL-5620/COL KOS 2031, CD: COL-CBS CK 32602/W.B. 3102-2)
A very dramatic show for advanced groups.

Carnival! (Tams-Witmark)

(MGM-39460C)
Good high school show. Easy to direct.

Carousel (Rodgers and Hammerstein Music Library) (1956)

(DC-9020/CAP W-694/RCA LOC-1114, CD: CAP 7 46635 2)
Another dramatic show with great music but for advanced groups.

Damn Yankees (Music Theatre International) (1958)

RCA LOC-1021/RCA LOC-1047/RCA AYL1-3948, CD: RCA)
A fun and easy show. A great show for male involvement.

The Fantasticks (Music Theatre International)

(MGM-38720C, CD: PolyGram 821, 943-2)
One of the best small cast shows. May have to cut rape number depending on your community.

Fiddler on the Roof (Music Theatre International) (1971, CBS/Fox Video)

(RCA LOC-1093/COL OL-6610/COL OS-3010, CD: RCA RCD1-7060)
A show needing a large cast. Many dramatic scenes. Show also relies on a strong male lead.

Finian's Rainbow (Tams-Witmark) (1968, Warner Home Video)

> (COL OL–4062/COL OS–2080/RCA LOC–1057, CD: COL–CBS CK 4062)
> Good music. Must have an equal number of white and black actors as show deals with racial equality.

Funny Girl (Tams-Witmark) (1968, RCA/Columbia Home Video)

> (CAP VAS–2059, CD: COL–CBS CK 3220/ CAP 7 46634 2)
> A great book and music. Show relies on a very strong and versatile female lead.

Godspell (Theatre Maximum)

> (BELL–1102)
> Great show with a strong Christian theme.

Grease (Samuel French) (1978, Paramount Home Video)

> (MGM 1 SE 34)
> A fun show for high school students because of the 1950s theme and the success of the film. May need to change some dialogue and words to music depending on your community.

Guys and Dolls (Music Theatre International) (1955, CBS/Fox Video)

> (DEC–9023/Motown M6–87651/MCA–1628)
> A great beginners' show. Easy to get males involved because of the masculine male gamblers.

Gypsy (Tams-Witmark) (1962, Warner Home Video)

> (COL OL–5420/COL OS–2017/WB–1480, CD: COL–CBS CK 32607)
> A great show for female actresses. May have to play down stripper theme and build on the domineering mother, which show is really about.

Hello, Dolly! (Tams-Witmark) (1969, CBS/Fox Video)

> (RCA LOCD–1087/RCA LOCD–2007/RCA LSO–1147, CD: RCA 3814–2 RG)
> Wonderful audience pleaser. Show relies on a very strong female character.

How to Succeed in Business without Really Trying (Music Theatre International) (1967)

> (RCA LOC- 1066/U.A.–4151/U.A.–5151)
> A great beginners' show. Easy to direct and fun to perform.

The King and I (Rodgers and Hammerstein Music Library) (1956, CBS/ Fox Video)

> (DEC–9088/RCA LOC–1092/CAP W–740)
> Many dramatic scenes. Needs to have experienced actors.

Li'l Abner (Tams-Whitmark) (1959)

> (COL OL–5150/COL OL- 5460/COL OS–2021)
> Fun show. Actors must physically resemble the cartoon characters.

Little Mary Sunshine (Metromedia)

> Good show that needs strong direction.

Little Shop of Horrors (Samuel French) (1986, Warner Home Video)

> (Geffen Records, CD: Geffen)
> A fun show for a small cast. An audience pleaser, much due to the success of the film. Script originally used both black and white actors but can be done with either. Puppet plants are available from several costume companies.

Mame (Tams-Witmark) (1974, Warner Home Video)

> (COL KOL–6600/COL KOS–3000, CD: COL-CBS CK 3000)
> Great Herman music. Requires numerous sets and very strong female lead characters.

The Music Man (Music Theatre International) (1961, Warner Home Video)

> (CAP SW–8–0990/W.B.- 1459, CD: CAP 7 46633 2/W.B. 1459–2)
> A great beginners' show and audience pleaser. Needs strong, experienced male actor.

My Fair Lady (Tams-Witmark) (1964, CBS/Fox Video)

> (COL OL–5090/COL OS–2015/COL KOL–8000/COL KOS–2600, CD: COL-CBS CK 5090)

A big show that should be attempted only by experienced groups.

No, No Nanette (Tams-Witmark)

(COL S–30563, CD: CK 30563)
Many good character parts and some great music.

Oklahoma! (Rodgers and Hammerstein Music Library) (1955, CBS/Fox Video)

(DEC–9017/CAP WAO–595, CD: CAP 466312)
A wonderful story and music. One of the most seen shows. Because everyone has seen Oklahoma!, your production may need to live up to what is expected.

Oliver! (Tams-Witmark) (1969, RCA/Columbia House Video)

(RCA LOCD–2004, CD: RCA 5501–2–R/RCA 4113–2RG)
Very dramatic show that needs several small boys. Difficult if girls try to play male roles.

Once Upon a Mattress (Music Theatre International)

(KAPP–4507/KAPP– 5507)
Fun show for beginners.

The Pajama Game (Music Theatre International) (1957)

(COL-OL–4840/COL OL–5210, CD: COL-CBS)
Good show but needs to be updated somewhat.

Seven Brides for Seven Brothers (Music Theatre International) (1954, MGM/UA Home Video)

(DRG DS–15025)
A fun show that follows the film almost word for word. Script needs some adapting to the stage.

Show Boat (Rodgers and Hammerstein Music Library) (1951, MGM/UA Home Video)

(COL OL- 4058/COL OL–5820/COL OS–2220/METRO–527 CD: COL-CBS CK 2220/EMI- Angel AZ–49108/Stanyan STZ 107–2)

A wonderful dramatic show with great music. Needs both white and black actors to bring across the underlying racial theme.

The Sound of Music (Rodgers and Hammerstein Music Library) (1965, CBS/Fox Video)

(COL KOL- 5450/COL LOS–2020/RCA LOCD–2005, CD: COL–CBS CK 32601/RCA PCD 1–2005)
Another show most people have seen. Should be done only if you can recreate the spectacle and grandeur.

South Pacific (Rodgers and Hammerstein Music Library) (1958, CBS/Fox Video)

(COL OL–4180/COL OS–2040/RCA LOC–1032, CD: COL–CBS CK 32604/RCA 3681–2-R)
Fun show that gives a large group of males much stage experience.

The Unsinkable Molly Brown (Tams-Witmark) (1984, MGM/UA Home Video)

(CAP W–2152/MGM–4232ST)
A somewhat weak show that relies on a female lead.

West Side Story (Music Theatre International) (1961, CBS/Fox Video)

(COL OL–5230/COL OL–2001/COL OL–5670/COL OL–2070, CD: COL-CBS CK 32603)
A very dramatic show that requires experienced male singers and dancers.

Where's Charley? (Music Theatre International) (1952)

(Monmouth-Evergreen-S7029)
A great show that is often overlooked. Fun for both the cast and audience.

The Wiz (Samuel French) (1978)

(Atlantic SD–18137/MCA 2–14000)
A show written for an all black cast but one that has been done successfully with both whites and blacks.

Working (Samuel French)

> (COL–35411)
> An easy show with great roles for inexperienced actors. A good show to start with and to develop characters.

You're a Good Man, Charlie Brown (Tams-Witmark)

> (MGM–S1E9)
> A good show for a small cast.

Since a musical usually requires a cast of at least 30 people who not only act but also sing and dance, it is important that you know you have the students to cast. In fairness, shows should never be precast; however, if you are planning to do a show like *Camelot, Funny Girl, Gypsy, Hello, Dolly!* or *The King and I,* you need to be assured that you have a student who can play King Arthur, Fanny Brice, Momma Rose, Dolly Levi, or The King of Siam. If you are not sure you have a student who can act, sing, and dance these parts, you should select another show or you may be committing professional suicide. On the positive side, you may have students attend auditions that you were not counting on and then will have to make a decision. Never put a student in a part in which he or she cannot be successful. Remember: We are working with inexperienced students. This is educational theatre—where students should be given the opportunity to *achieve,* not be embarrassed.

Companies holding performance rights to shows will send perusal copies usually for a two-week period (you paying the cost of shipping). Some companies will supply you with forms for this purpose; however, most companies will readily send perusal copies if you request them on your school or department letterhead. Once you have selected a show and completed your contract, you are free to keep the perusal copies of your selected show so that you can begin audition preparations.

14

Supply Companies

Hundreds of companies offer theatre supplies for sale. Each has its unique way of displaying pricing and instructions for ordering. In 13 years of teaching and directing, I have read catalogs from, ordered from, and worked with many of these companies. Following is an annotated list of suppliers who I feel offer the best service, prices, and products.

BUTTONS

Continental Press Printing Ideas
34 N.E. Riverside Dr.
Box 1063
St. Cloud, MN 56302
612–251–5876

The service is fast and the prices are competitive. They will allow you to charge after receiving a signed purchase order. The customer service department is very friendly and helpful. Send for a catalog.

COSTUMES

The Tuxedo Wholesaler
7750 E. Redfield Rd., Suite 101
Scottsdale, AZ 85260
602–951–1606

Very friendly and helpful people. They primarily offer period suits for men. The suits are packed well for shipment and you can normally get things quickly. Some prices are higher than what most high school budgets can afford. Great catalog. Remember: We make our own costumes, which means we do not require the services of many costume companies (see Chapter 7).

DROPS

Fullerton Civic Light Opera
218 W. Commonwealth Avenue
Fullerton, CA 92632
714–992–0710 (drops)
714–879–9761 (costumes)

This organization has both drops and costumes available for rental. The drops and costumes have been designed and used in their own productions. A drop catalogue is available, which shows the drops along with listing color and size. Both departments are friendly and helpful. Cost breaks are also given on additional weeks' rental and for renting entire shows.

Kenmark Scenic Studio
4460 Arville #5
Las Vegas, NV 89103
702–873–2003

A relatively new company but already in the forefront of the rental drop business. Most drops are newly painted and available for most shows. A great company with which to work. They stand behind their product and service. If they don't have what you want, they will go out of their way to accommodate you. They have no drop catalog but will send color pictures of available drops. This company also rents props and set pieces to be used mainly for dance recitals, proms, and conventions; however, many are suitable for stage shows. They also design and build shows for professional companies, which in most cases would be well out of price range for high schools. They do offer a prop catalog that includes individual descriptions of the available props for rent. They will also send pictures of any prop you are interested in renting. If you are looking to rent drops, call this studio first.

Schell Scenic Studio
841 South Front Street
Columbus, OH 43206
614–444–9550

This is an older company that deals in older drops. Recently they
have begun to paint new drops of their old designs; I have found these
to be very well done. The older drops are well used and vary in size;
they will, however, fold and pin drops to fit your needs. The service
and friendliness here is outstanding. They have a new catalog with pictures and narrative on all their drops, draperies, and equipment. There
is a small charge for the catalog but it is well worth having. Normally
this is the most reasonable drop company. Cost breaks are given for
multiple rental weeks, which most drop companies will not do. It is
worth a try, but be aware of the older drops and the varying sizes.

Charles H. Stewart & Company
6–8 Claredon Avenue
Somerville, MA 02144
617–625–2407

This company has some very nice drops, many of which work well
on the smaller high school stage. Their prices are competitive, but their
service leaves a lot to be desired. When using this company I always
send my order to them in writing several times and make several calls
to see that drops will arrive when needed. The customer shouldn't have
to do this. They print a catalog with some pictures and a short narrative
of all available drops.

Tobins Lake Studio
7030 Old US 23
Brighton, MI 48166
313–229–6666

Some of the nicest drops can be found at this company. The problem, however, is that you must order very early because you may find
the ones you want have already been reserved by someone else for your
dates. They are very friendly and helpful. Their packing and shipping
of the drops may be one of the best. You should expect to pay more for
their drops, and it seems their prices continue to climb. They have a
well illustrated and informative catalog and will send color photos of
drops at a small additional cost. You will be satisfied with the company
but may pay more.

MISCELLANEOUS PROPS AND SUPPLIES

Anderson's
5350 N. Hwy. 61
White Bear Lake, MN 55110
1-800-328-9640

This company specializes in prom decorations, some of which are suitable for backdrops or set decorations. Most everything is made of paper and therefore may need additional reinforcement, which you must provide. Most items are made to be used only one night and not for several weeks of a production. They also make the assembly sound easy but in reality is usually very difficult. Many of the items are expensive but if you are running short of time or are working by yourself, this company may be able to help.

Two other companies who deal in prom materials and are much like Anderson's are:

Prom Nite
P.O. Box 10833
St. Paul, MN 55110
1-800-642-1081

and

Stumps
Box 305
South Whitley, IN 46787-0305
1-800-992-9251

American Display Co.
P.O. Box 689, 43694
119 N. Ontario St.
Toledo, OH 43624

Very friendly and helpful service. This company mainly deals in paper products. Most of their items are divided by theme. A majority of their business is parties, proms, and conventions. They do have some three-dimensional props. A catalog of most of their paper products is available. Call or write for a catalog.

Johnson Smith Company
35075 Automation Drive
Mt. Clemens, MI 48043
313-791-2805

This company's catalog is filled with crazy and outrageous items. They are a good source for hard-to-find props.

Paper Warehouse
9559 Nall Ave.
Overland Park, KS
913-341-5700

Another fun store loaded with almost every theme item imaginable. They have many things that can be used as props or for set decoration. Items are reasonably priced in case you need to demolish your set due to lack of storage.

Oriental Merchandise Company, Inc.
2636 Edenborn Ave.
Metairie, LA 70002
1-800-535-7335

Another company that deals in novelty supplies. They have items that can be used as set decorations if you are doing a play with an oriental plot or setting. They offer a toll-free order number.

Theatre House, Inc.
P.O. Box 2090
400 W. Third Street
Covington, KY 41012-2090
600-431-2414

The ordering department is very friendly here. The service is very good and you can normally receive your merchandise quickly. Do check carefully after you receive an item because you may find it is not as it appeared in their illustrating catalog. The colored catalog is divided according to periods. They will allow you to return items after receiving an authorization number but may charge a restocking fee. They deal in novelties, makeup, costumes, lighting, and so on. The costumes, however, are very expensive and are poorly constructed. For makeup and small props or costume accessories, give this company a try. They offer fast service and will allow you to charge over the phone with a purchase order number.

U.S. Toy Company
1227 E. 119
Kansas City, MO
816–761–5900

A fine source for novelty items, props, costume accessories, and magic supplies. They will ship but require a purchase order number. You may order by phone. A catalog is available and outlines most of their products. If you need to buy in large quantities, this is the place. Call for a catalog.

PUBLICITY

Package Publicity Service, Inc.
1501 Broadway
New York, NY 10036
212–354–1840

If you need quick information for press releases and director notes, this may be the company you want to contact. They will allow you to charge and will take your order over the phone. They are a good resource for advertising logotypes. The pressbooks are not always up-to-date and many times do include typographic and grammar errors. You can still usually find enough information to use from the pressbooks. They offer a catalog that lists a large number of shows. Stock buttons, posters, postcards, and T-shirts are also available. Prices are competitive.

RECORDS AND COMPACT DISCS

Rose Records
214 South Wabash
Chicago, IL 60604

When looking for original Broadway soundtrack recordings on either record or compact disc, this company may be your best source.

They send out a catalogue about four or five times a year, usually with a section devoted to Broadway, London, and movie musicals. The best thing about this company is its prices—some of the most reasonable I have found. If you do not find what you are looking for in the catalogue, they may still be able to get it for you at a substantial savings.

SCRIPTS: PLAY/MUSICAL

For the most part, the following companies are equal in service and merchandise. Normally only one company will hold the performance rights to a certain play or musical, so you may not have much choice of which company to use.

Baker's Plays
100 Chauncy Street
Boston, MA 02111
617–482–1280

Dramatists Play Service, Inc.
723 Seventh Ave.
New York, NY 10019
212–944–0595

The Dramatic Publishing Company
P.O. Box 109
Woodstock, IL 60098
815–338–7170

Samuel French, Inc.
45 W. 25th St.
New York, NY 10010
212–206–8990

Metromedia On Stage
1700 Broadway
New York, NY 10019

Musical Theatre International
545 Eighth Avenue
New York, NY 10018
212–868–6668

Rodgers & Hammerstein Theatre Library
598 Madison Ave.
New York, NY 10022
212–486–0643

Tams-Witmark Music Library, Inc.
580 Lexington Avenue
New York, NY 10022
1–800–221–7196

Theatre Maximus
New York, NY
212–765–5913

SETS

Rollerwall Inc.
P.O. Box 757
Silver Spring, MD 20901
301–589–5516

If you want a fast, easy, and authentic way to reproduce wallpaper on a set, then you must see this company's product. You may find the initial investment high, but the final result should make up for it. They will not accept orders over the phone. You must send in the order with a purchase order number or on a letterhead. Make sure you order well in advance, as they are slow and will charge extra for rush service. To give your set a look that will certainly bring compliments and save you time, call for a catalog.

TICKETS

Ticket Craft
1925 Bellmore Avenue
Bellmore, NY 11710
1–800–645–4944

If you have a large house and several productions per year, then I would suggest you have this company print your tickets. Once you have sent them the floor plan of your house, it is easy to order tickets because you are already in their computer. The cost of the tickets may be more than you would pay locally, but you will not have to number them and they will look very professional. This is the same company from which I purchase ticket envelopes. Very friendly people. They normally will offer a 15 percent discount off your first order and they have a toll-free number. If you want professional looking tickets and don't mind paying for them, call this company (see Chapter 9).

THEATRE BOOKS FOR PURCHASE

The Fireside Theatre
Customer Service Center
501 Franklin Avenue
Garden City, NY 11530

This is a theatre book club that sends you information on a featured selection about once every month. I used this club for years to build my script library and resource center. The books are reasonably priced. The great thing about this company is that they will keep you up-to-date with the latest script offerings. When a show opens on Broadway, you can bet it will be next week's featured selection.

Publishers Central Bureau
One Champion Ave./Dept. 483
Avenel, NJ 07001–2301
1–800-PCB-9800. Ext. 483

This is a fine company that offers theatre and general entertainment books for drastically low prices. They offer a free catalog that is sent about every month. Included in the catalog are books on architecture, good for set design research, and paper dolls books, good for costume research. A large portion of the catalog is devoted to videos and records. If you wish to build a theatre or film library either at home or at school, this company is your best bet. Scripts are generally not available through this company.

TROPHIES AND AWARDS

Dinn Brothers (Trophies)
68 Winter Street
P.O. Box 111
Holyoke, MA 01041
1-800-628-9657

If you are in need of any type of an award, trophy, plaque, or medal, then this company can supply it. They offer a free engraving policy along with a toll-free number for ordering. The cost is the best part of this company. I have never found more reasonably priced awards. They guarantee their product and will make corrections if needed. If you give drama or speech awards or need medals and trophies for a play festival or forensic contest, you must call for a catalog.

VIDEOCASSETTES

You can rent videos of plays and musicals that have been made into films at your local video store, as most stores provide a good selection. Following are the main distributors of musical videos:

CBS/Fox Video
39000 Seven Mile Rd.
Livonia, MI 48152

Karl-Lorimar Home Video, Inc.
17942 Cowan
Irvine, CA 92714
and
70 The Esplanade
Toronto, Ontario, Canada MSE1R2

MCA Home Video
70 Universal City Plaza
Universal City, CA 91608

MGM/UA Home Video
1350 Avenue of the Americas
New York, NY 10019

Paramount Home Video
5555 Melrose Ave.
Hollywood, CA 90038

Warner Home Video, Inc.
4000 Warner Blvd.
Burbank, CA 91522

15

Magazines and Publications

It is important that directors keep up with new theatrical works and current happenings in both the educational and professional theatre. There are several publications that are well suited for this purpose and lend themselves to quick and easy reading. Publications that you use directly for your work are tax deductible as business expenses. You may also want to request that your school library subscribe to one or more theatre publications. If this is impossible, you should prepare a small library or resource center in your classroom, making the materials available to your students on a check-out basis. Publications are also a good resource for supplemental materials for the classroom. Attempt to store all of your back issues of magazines, as you will find that you will refer to them often.

Back Stage

330 West 42nd St.
New York, NY 10036
212–947–0020
fax: 212–967–6786

This is a very informative newspaper-type publication devoted to stage, film, and casting. As you keep up with current happenings around the country, your students will see what professional companies expect when holding auditions and what type of jobs are available and where. A generous amount of ads for speech and voice, dance, acting lessons, resumés, and photography services are included. This is a weekly publication.

Dramatics

Educational Theatre Association
3368 Central Parkway
Cincinnati, OH 45225
513–559–1996

This publication is published for members of the International Thespian Society and the Theatre Education Association; however, you do not need to be a member of these organizations to receive a subscription. This is one of the few magazines published for both secondary directors and students. Since many colleges and universities advertise here, this is one of the best sources for students to receive college information. A Reader Service Card is made available in each issue. Helpful stagecraft hints are often included and are useful to any size program. Published monthly except in June, July, and August.

Playbill

Playbill Inc.
71 Vanderbilt Ave.
New York, NY 10169

If you like to stay abreast of the happenings on Broadway and London, then you may want to take a look at this publication. This monthly publication is fashioned after the Broadway Playbill or program. Because of its monthly publication, some information may be outdated by the time it reaches your mailbox. Still, this is a fun and interesting magazine to receive.

Theatre Crafts

Theatre Crafts Associates
135 Fifth Avenue
New York, NY 10010–7193
212–677–5997

This publication is written more for the professional and university audience. However, it has many interesting articles on theatres from around the country and will keep you updated on what is happening in professional theatre. This monthly magazine is a good resource for supplies and for university theatre programs. It contains many colored pictures and it features many articles on costuming and scene design. Many production pictures enhance the articles and serve as great references. A Reader Service Card for receiving more information about services and schools can be found in each issue.

Theatre Week

That New Magazine
28 West 25th Street, 4th Floor
New York, NY 10010
212–627–2120

This is one of my favorite magazines. If you want up-to-date information on the Broadway theatre, a subscription to *Theatre Week* is a must. After a show opens on Broadway, the magazine includes the highlights from all major reviews, along with the magazine's own review. Different shows and performers are featured in the weekly articles. Many times, lists of performers' and directors' shows are included and serve as historical backgrounds. A special issue each year is devoted to the Tonys. A *Theatre Week* Listings is in every issue, which gives all shows playing on Broadway, Off Broadway and Off Off Broadway for that week.

Show Music

P.O. Box A
East Haddam, CT 06423–0218
203–873–8664

I have watched this magazine go from a newsletter format to the country's premiere show music publication. This magazine is full of interesting articles and beautiful reproduced photos of artists, rehearsals, and casts. Along with articles on show music, information is included on CDs and videocassettes. The only problem is that it is published only four times a year—but the wait for the next issue only makes it more exciting. The features on individual performers are extensive. Beginning in 1991, *Show Music* will be published by the Goodspeed Opera House. Max O. Preeo will remain editor and have access to the large archive of scores, sheet music, scripts, sound recordings, books, theatre programs, and memorabilia housed at Goodspeed. Again, this makes a great resource for any library. If you love musical theatre, then this publication is a must.

16

Final Curtain

This chapter contains miscellaneous information that does not need an entire chapter devoted to each subject. However, some of the most important and helpful information to make your job a little easier may be found here.

USING DROPS WITHOUT FLY SPACE

Many directors around the country find themselves presenting productions in less than adequate surroundings. Performance spaces may consist of a classroom, lecture hall, gym, cafeteria, or at least a stage that is not equipped with fly space. The good news is that in all of these areas you can still use painted drops.

One way is to secure a pipe from the ceiling with rope or chain. This is easy if you are working in a room with an open ceiling, as you simply tie the rope to the pipe, throw the rope over the rafters, and hoist the pipe up. Your maintenance department will have old pipe that can be used for this purpose. Pipe that is 2 to 3 inches in diameter is best; don't use pipe that is too heavy, as it will require more safety lines. A line should be placed about every 8 to 10 feet and on both ends. The lines can then be tied to stage weights or cement blocks placed on the floor behind the overhead pipe. Most gyms will have places on the walls from which you can secure the ropes. Unless you are able to lower and raise the pipe during the production, this method may limit you to using only one drop.

Another way to use more than one drop in a production without fly space is to hang a two-way traveler track over your performance area. These tracks can be ordered in the desired length and can be rented or purchased. I found that purchasing a track paid for itself over the years.

Once the track is secured, usually with chain, tie the drop on "carriers" that run on the track. The drop is then manually pulled from stage right to stage left and back again. Two drops can easily be tied on each track. I have put as many as four drops on a track, but this requires additional chain lines.

The average drop is between 40 and 45 feet wide. If your performance area cannot accommodate a drop of this size, depending on the drop, you can fold the sides back, tying them on the pipe or carriers as you would with the rest of the drop. Most drops are 18 to 21 feet high. However, many companies have a few drops that are 10, 15, or 16 feet high. You will have to do some calling to find the smaller drops, but they can be found. (See Chapter 14 for a list of drop companies.) Do not pin, staple, or put nails in drops, for you will probably end up regretting it.

FINDING PAINT

If you find that theatrical scene paint is too expensive, scenery can be painted with latex paint. Indoor, outdoor, or even porch paint is usable as long as it is latex.

Your best source for paint is stores that have paint that was mixed and not picked up by the customer. Once paint has been mixed, it is virtually unsellable. Upon knowing what you will be doing with the paint, many stores will either give you the paint as a tax write-off or sell it to you at a very reasonable rate. I call the paint stores in our area twice a year; as a result, I get between 50 to 100 gallons of paint per store free or for 10 to 15 percent of the cost.

Another source for paint is your school district. Most districts receive a school cost that is much lower than buying paint over the counter. Some districts purchase what is known as "prison paint" because it is made at the state prison and is very inexpensive.

COURSE DESCRIPTIONS

If you are called upon to add speech and theatre courses to the curriculum, you will need to write a course description. Following are sample descriptions that may help you in this process.

Acting I: Grades 10–11; one semester. This course is for the beginning performer. Mime, improvisation, comedy, drama, and one-act performances will be emphasized. Students will be required to memorize dialogue for presentation in class.

Acting II: Grades 10–12; one semester. This is a performance course for specialization in various acting techniques. Musical comedy, children's theatre, comedy, drama, and mime will be studied in more depth, as a continuation of Acting I. Students will be required to memorize dialogue for presentation in class.

Business Speech: Grades 10–12; one semester. This course is for the student who is considering a career in the field of business. Speech topics related to business such as problem solving, group discussions, and planning and multimedia presentations will be studied. Students will be required to complete and present projects throughout the course.

Directing: Grades 11–12; one year; prerequisite—Acting I and Audition. This year-long course is designed to give the performer more experience in front of a variety of audiences. The student must audition for a position in the class. The class will perform at various community events, both during and after school. Outside performances are required as part of the course.

Drama: Grades 9–12; one semester; prerequisite—permission of instructor. This will be a survey course that includes study of the historical backgrounds of drama, plays, and play production. Some of the classwork will be done in conjunction with productions presented by the theatre department; other aspects will evolve from projects in the class, ranging from acting to technical theatre, depending on the interests of the individual.

Films of the 30s, 40s, 50s: Grades 9–12; one semester; prerequisite—permission of instructor. This will be survey course that will include a look at the films, actors, and directors of the 30s, 40s, and 50s that influenced and helped shape our society. The course will include critical reviews of select films from the periods and research of actors, actresses, and directors who starred in them.

Forensics I & II: Grades 10–12; one semester; prerequisite—permission of instructor. This course is designed to provide the individual student with development of talents in public speaking and interpretive events. Individual instruction in extemporaneous speaking, informative speaking, oratory, prose and poetry interpretation, dramatic and humorous interpretive readings, and impromptu speaking. Students are given the opportunity and urged to participate in tournament competition at various levels.

Practical Speech I: Grades 9–12. This class will cover the same materials as Speech I; however, it will be geared to those students who are being required to repeat Speech I.

Radio, TV, & Film: Grades 9–12; one semester; prerequisite—Speech I and permission of instructor. The class will focus on radio, television and film history, promotion, editorials, sports, commentaries, programming, directing, and on-air delivery. Course work will include the writing, producing, and filming of a weekly news program for broadcast to the student body.

Repertory Theatre: Grades 11–12; one year; prerequisite—Acting I and Audition. This year-long course is designed to give the performer more experience in front of a variety of audiences. The student must audition for a position in the class. The class will perform at various community events, both during and after school. Outside performances are required as part of the course.

Speech I: Grades 9–12; one semester. The purpose of this course is to acquaint the student with the fundamentals of speech, help him or her acquire confidence through maximum speaking experiences before people, and awaken the students to the need for speaking ability in all aspects of life. With the successful completion of this course, the student should be able to use basic speaking techniques, give and accept constructive criticism, research and analyze information, demonstrate listening skills, use basic research techniques, use basic techniques of effective delivery, organize a body of information in logical patterns of organization, and identify the importance of nonverbal communication.

Speech II: Grades 9–12; one semester; prerequisite—Speech I and permission of instructor. This course is a continuation of the speaking skills learned in Speech I. Emphasis is placed on some of the more specific skills in speaking and continued opportunities are provided for the student to speak effectively in formal and informal situations. Interpersonal communication, goals of communication, and the process of communication events for specific areas of performance both in and out of the classroom. Strong emphasis is placed on logical and persuasive arguments.

Stagecraft I & II: Grades 9–12; one semester; prerequisite—permission of instructor. This course is a study of the basic aspects of technical theatre production with emphasis on construction techniques for theatrical settings. The area of costuming, makeup, lighting, and properties are also studied, along with various other phases of technical theatre. Some work outside of class is required, mostly in conjunction with the plays produced during the semester.

STAGE BLOOD

It is very easy to make stage blood: Simply mix together red food coloring, Karo syrup, and water. Mix the syrup and water together to get the desired consistency and then add color.

If a character is to be knifed, a plastic bag or a balloon filled with the stage blood can be taped to the knifed area under the actor's costume (as in *Dial "M" for Murder*). Be sure to round the corners of the knife or scissors so as not to hurt the actor. If the actor is to be shot, he or she simply pushes against the bag or balloon.

If blood is to appear on the character as he or she is cut, run a small tube down the length of the knife and place a small ball of blood in the handle of the knife. When the stabber squeezes on the handle and simultaneously runs the knife over the character, it will appear as if the character is bleeding while being cut.

MAKING PERIOD DOCUMENTS

To make a period document, brush coffee or tea over the paper, which will give the paper a brown, worn look. Then take the paper and lay it on a cookie sheet and place it in the oven for about 30 seconds, watching to see that it does not burn. You may also want to cut or burn the edges of the paper to give it an authentic look.

DINNER THEATRE

Planning and serving a dinner theatre can be both fun and profitable. However, it takes much planning and organization. The first thing you, as the director, should do is get a group or person to handle the purchasing and preparing of the meal. Suggestions might be the district food supervisor, the drama club with parent leadership, or an outside catering group (the catering group may increase your costs).

Dinner reservations are a must. Print and number tickets for both adults and students. If you are selling reserved theatre tickets, you will need a separate ticket for the show and dinner. Make a diagram of your dining room and place people at tables as you sell tickets. Make a master list with name, table, ticket number, and the adult and student count per table. This will help in seating the people the night of the dinner (see Figure 16.1).

The dining area should be dimly lit and the tables should be covered with linen table cloths. Most schools have a regular linen service that will rent these to you. Never use plastic table service. Decorate the tables and, if possible, play taped music from the show. A program from the show could be placed at each table setting, which will give people something to do as they wait for their meal. Show props and other pieces of scenery can be used in the dining area to add atmosphere.

The meal should include a salad bar, meat, potato, rolls, and dessert. A cheese and cracker appetizer might also be offered. The salad bar can consist of a tossed salad with all the fixings, or individual people could donate different types of salads. Baked potatoes work well and are easy to prepare, but twice-baked potatoes and wild rice are very popular. The meat needs to be pre-cut portions. It might be baked chicken, roast beef, Cornish game hens, or Chicken Cordon Bleu. The plate's appearance is helped by laying the meat on a piece of lettuce, adding a slice of orange or candied apple, or covering the meat with a sauce. A choice of desserts always seems to work well. Suggested desserts are cheesecake, cobbler, or cake. A choice of drinks should also be offered. Iced tea is often a favorite, along with milk and coffee.

It is also interesting to name menu items after characters in the show. The menu flier should be made and included in all your mailings (see Figures 16.2 and 16.3).

A person should serve as a host or hostess to greet people and show them to their tables. One server should be assigned to no more than three to four tables. Servers can dress in costume or you can have all wear white shirts and black pants or skirts.

Servers should be briefed on the proper way to wait on tables. You might give your servers a list of dinner theatre instructions like the following:

Serve from the right and take from the left.

1. Fill water glasses during the following—"Hello. Welcome to our dinner theatre. My name is _____. If there is any thing I can get to make your evening more enjoyable, please ask."
2. "I would first like to take your drink order. We have coffee, iced tea, or milk." (Start in one place and go around the table.)
3. "I will bring your salad plates and you may begin with the salad bar."
4. After they have finished their salads you will remove the salad plates and bring the guests their dinner.
5. After they eat their dinner you will remove their plates and bring them dessert.

6. After they have eaten their dessert you will remove the dessert plates. Ask them if there is anything else you can get them, then tell them to enjoy the show.
7. Keep water glasses filled at all times.

Never let the servers eat without paying; they should eat at cost so as not to cut into your profits.

Dinner theatre can be fun and profitable if it is organized well.

FIELD TRIPS

One of the best ways to generate interest in theatre is to have your students see other theatrical productions. Professional or college theatre is best; however, secondary theatre directors should support and encourage each other by attending other high school productions. I once had a student ask me, "Is there music in a musical?" This is the most extreme case of a student being unfamiliar with theatre. Students need to know that there are others out there doing the same thing they are.

A theatre trip to New York will give your students an unbelievable boost. While teaching in Ohio, my drama club visited New York City every Thanksgiving. There were never any problems and several adult trips were taken because of the success of the student trips. There are several package trips that you can take or you can put together your own trip by working with your local travel agent.

All 50 states have film commissions or an agency that facilitates filming in their state. Call your state commission to see what projects are planned in your area. The film commission can arrange a time for your students to visit the set and to talk with the actors and production staff.

Before any field trip is taken you will need to have a permission form. Check to see if your school has a standard form; if not, you can make your own by using the following example:

I give my permission for _____
                                                    STUDENT NAME

to attend the performance of *Oliver!* on the State University campus, Wednesday, October 19. All students will be transported by school bus and will be leaving Central High School at 9:00 a.m. and returning about 5:00 p.m. I further understand that he/she will need to have money for lunch at the University Union.

_____   _____
PARENT/GUARDIAN SIGNATURE   DATE

I, _____, have contacted
all of my teachers in advance of attending *Oliver!* at State University,
Wednesday, October 19, and have made up or will make up all
missed class work. While on this field trip I agree to conduct myself
in a mature manner and be a fine representative of Central High
School.

_____   _____

BASIC SCENERY

Since the building of scenery will vary from production to production
and from performance area to performance area, it may be helpful to
compile a list of basic scenery that all departments can use, such as:

1. 2–3 door flats
2. 2–3 window flats
3. 1 fireplace flat
4. 1 archway flat
5. 2–3 flats, 2–4–6 feet wide
6. 2–4 platforms, 4 × 8
7. 2 platforms, 2 × 8

Keep in mind that by adding 3-inch castor wheels to the platforms,
you will have a wagon. One prop that is easy to build and that will get
a lot of use is a bench. The same bench can be used in the train scene
of the *Music Man* by adding a train seatfront cut from plywood and
painted, a garden scene in *Once Upon a Mattress* by adding a scalloped
boarder, and so on. The benches are made from 1 × 10 and 1 × 1 lum-
ber (see Figure 16.4).

Two of the best sources for building high school scenery are *Essen-
tials of Stage Scenery* by Samuel Selden and Tom Rezzuto (Appleton-
Century-Crofts, Educational Division, Meredith Corporation) and *The
Theatre Student Scenery* by W. Joseph Stell (Richards Rosen Press, Inc.).

FLOORING AND PLANKING

A fast and easy way to make a platform appear as if it is a plank floor
is to cut pieces of wood one inch wide off the edge of different sized

boards. You then take these cuttings, which normally would be thrown away, and glue them on the top edge of the platform about one inch apart. You paint between the cuttings and line your "planks" on the platform. This technique is useful in making the wharf for *Carousel* or the cabin floor for *Seven Brides for Seven Brothers* (see Figure 16.5).

Figure 16.6 presents photos from various high school productions. All sets in these photos were built by high school students. Perhaps these photos will generate creative scenery for your next production.

THEATRE HANDBOOK

Every theatre department should have a theatre handbook, which will be helpful to both students and parents in understanding what is expected through their participation in the department. Included in the handbook should be an attendance policy, audition policy, costume construction and loan procedures, field trip policies, and any other information needed to be a successful participant. If the theatre director is also the forensic director, the information for both departments could be combined. The handbook should begin with an introduction by the director. The excerpts in Figure 16.7 may serve as a guideline.

FRIDAY PERFORMANCE

Name and Table	Ticket #	Adults	Children
Table 1 (8)			
Alfie Thompson	107–113	4	3
Mary (H.E.L.P. Services)	183	1	0
Table 2 (7)			
Eileen Hertzler	184–188	5	0
Geraldine Hertzler	193–194	2	0
Table 3 (8)			
Jon Buckman	168–171	4	0
Braucksieck	211–213	2	1
Table 4 (5)			
Shirley Strack	137–141	5	0
Table 5 (6)			
Harold Wolf	150–155	6	0
Table 6 (5)			
Betty Smith	156–158	3	0
Dan Smith	220–221	2	0
Table 7 (5)			
Dr. George	127–132	4	2
Table 8 (5)			
Ann Hunsicker	158–163	4	1
Table 9 (5)			
Joyce O'Conner	228–232	2	3
Table 10 (6)			
Lloyd Lynn	209–210	2	0
Lloyd Lynn	133–136	2	2

FIGURE 16.1   Dinner theatre reservations.

DAMN YANKEES
PRE-SHOW DINNER

You and your family are invited to enjoy a delicious candlelight dinner before enjoying the very funny musical, *Damn Yankees.*

You will be guests of the AHS Theatre Department as they serve your party at your own table.

MENU:
Cheese and Crackers Appetizer

Salad Bar:
    fresh greens, croutons, bacon bits, cheese, eggs, carrots, celery, pickle spears, chow mein noodles, sunflower seeds
    Thousand Island, Ranch, or Italian dressings

Chicken Cordon Bleu

Sugar Snap Peas

Wild Rice or Baked Potato

Yankee's Delight

Hot Whole Wheat and White Rolls

Milk, Iced Tea, or Coffee

COST
$6.25 for Adults
$4.00 for Children under 12

Serving is from 6:00–7:00 p.m. The number of tickets is limited. Ticket sales end Tuesday, November 11, or when sold out.

For reservations, visit or call the high school library at 988–555–7101, Ext. 248

FIGURE 16.2   Dinner theatre menu.

GUYS AND DOLLS
PRE-SHOW DINNER

You and your family are invited to enjoy a delicious candlelight dinner before enjoying the very funny musical, *Guys and Dolls.*

You will be guests of the BHS Drama Club as they serve your party at your own table.

MENU:
Cheese and Crackers Appetizer

Salad Bar:
  fresh greens, croutons, bacon bits, cheese, eggs, carrots, celery, pickle spears, chow mein noodles, sunflower seeds
  Thousand Island, Ranch, or Italian dressings

Cornish Game Hen

French-Cut Green Beans Amandine

Baked Potato—Sour Cream/Butter

Cherry or Blueberry Cheesecake or Carrot Cake

Hot Whole Wheat and White Rolls

Milk, Iced Tea, or Coffee

COST
$5.75 for Adults
$3.25 for Children under 12

Serving is from 6:00–7:00 p.m. The number of tickets is limited. Ticket sales end Tuesday, April 12, or when sold out.

For reservations, visit or call the high school office at 368-555-1234, Ext. 210

FIGURE 16.3   Dinner theatre menu.

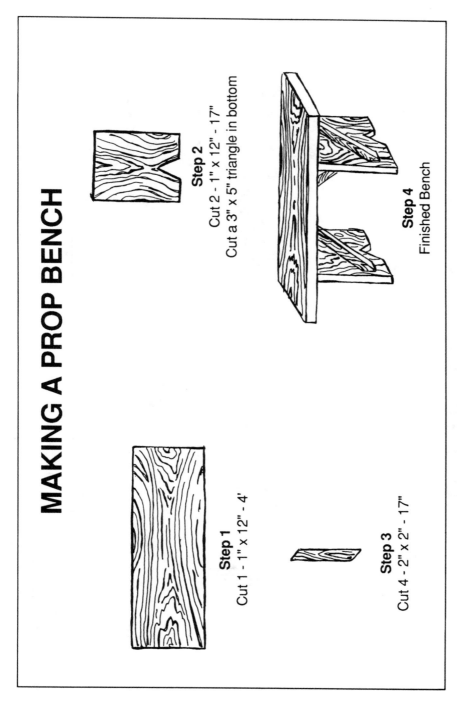

FIGURE 16.4   Materials and steps to build a prop bench. (Drawings by Eric Tow)

237

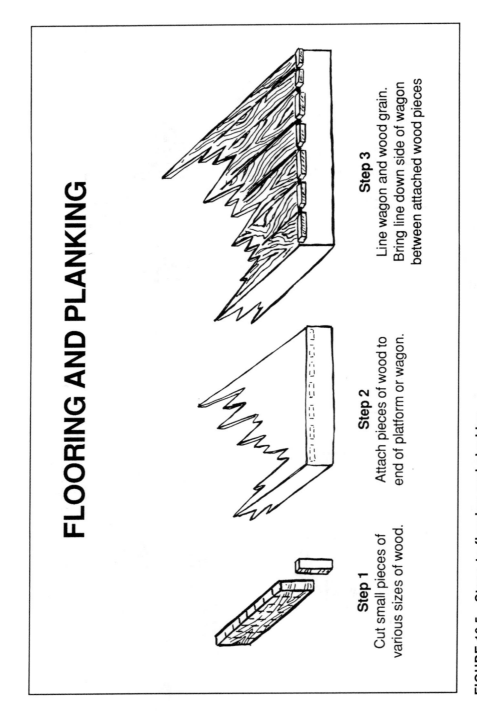

FLOORING AND PLANKING

Step 1
Cut small pieces of
various sizes of wood.

Step 2
Attach pieces of wood to
end of platform or wagon.

Step 3
Line wagon and wood grain.
Bring line down side of wagon
between attached wood pieces

**FIGURE 16.5   Steps to flooring and planking.
(Drawing by Eric Tow)**

FIGURE 16.6a *How to Succeed in Business Without Really Trying,* Clyde Senior High School, Clyde, Ohio. Back drop from Schell Scenic Studio, Columbus, Ohio.

FIGURE 16.6b *Dial "M" for Murder,* Gardner Edgerton High School, Gardner, Kansas. The flats were painted with a solid base color. The wallpaper was then rolled on, using rollers from Rollerwall.

FIGURE 16.6   Production photos.

FIGURE 16.6c *Frankenstein,* Olathe South High School, Olathe, Kansas.
The walls were painted with the rag-rolling method to give a period look.
Books in the bookcase are painted styrofoam fronts. (Courtesy of
Brett Stacks)

FIGURE 16.6d *And Miss Reardon Drinks a Little,* Gardner Edgerton High
School, Gardner, Kansas. The flats were painted with a solid base color.
The wallpaper was then rolled on, using rollers from Rollerwall.

FIGURE 16.6 Continued.

FIGURE 16.6e *Seven Brides for Seven Brothers,* Olathe South High School, Olathe, Kansas. Cabin is built on wagons that divide into three sections. Drop from Schell Scenic Studio, Columbus, Ohio. (Courtesy of Brett Stacks)

FIGURE 16.6f *Seven Brides for Seven Brothers,* Olathe South High School, Olathe, Kansas. Drop from Schell Scenic Studio, Columbus, Ohio. (Courtesy of Brett Stacks)

FIGURE 16.6 Continued.

FIGURE 16.6g   *Arsenic and Old Lace,* Clyde Senior High School, Clyde, Ohio. The flats were painted with a solid base color. The wallpaper was then rolled on, using rollers from Rollerwall.

FIGURE 16.6   Continued.

FROM THE DIRECTOR OF SPEECH AND THEATRE

The MHS Speech and Theatre Department is dedicated to excellence through the performing arts. Our purpose is to continue the tradition of outstanding educational theatre and forensics.

With any successful program there are always rules and regulations to help the program run smoothly. Within these pages are those rules and regulations that I hope you find will make your participation more enjoyable and rewarding.

I encourage all students and parents to read and familiarize themselves with this booklet. As always, parent support is vital to our success.

I look forward to your participation and your growth through the MHS Speech and Theatre Department.

James R. Opelt
Director of Speech and Theatre

TABLE OF CONTENTS (each with corresponding page numbers)

AUDITIONS

All auditions are opened to the entire school. Students without experience are encouraged to audition.

Auditions will be of the closed nature. Results of auditions are final. Any student who, after being cast in a production, quits that production may not audition for another show during that season (school year).

(continued)

FIGURE 16.7   Excerpts from theatre handbook.

Audition sign-ups will occur approximately 1 to 2 weeks before auditions. At that time, students will select an audition time and receive more information about auditioning.

COSTUME CONSTRUCTION

Cast members are responsible to construct or pay for the construction of their costumes. Material will be supplied by the MHS Theatre Department. All costumes become property of the MHS Theatre Department after the production.

Cast members will be responsible to bring all of their finished costumes to rehearsal when requested and treat them as their personal property.

COSTUME LOAN

Costumes are loaned to students for use in other classes but not for activities outside of school. Costumes are, however, rented to other high schools, community theatres, and universities.

CREW SIGN-UP

Crew sign-up will be held before each production. Crews will consist of stage, props, costumes, lights, sound, and costumes. Crews will vary from production to production.

FOOD IN AUDITORIUM

No food or drink is allowed in the auditorium, light booth, or on stage or in dressing rooms during a rehearsal, work session, or performance. All food and drink shall remain in the commons area. Failure to do this could result in a detention. (Food used in a production is permissible.)

FORENSIC LETTER AWARD CRITERIA

To be eligible for a letter in forensics the student must meet the following criteria:

1. The student must perform in two separate events each year.
2. The student must attend *all* scheduled tournaments including league, regional, and state festivals.

The following exceptions will still enable the student to fulfill this criteria:

a. Absence from a tournament due to a death in the family.
b. Absence from school due to illness.

To be excused, the student's parent must make personal contact with the forensics director before the scheduled tournament.

FIGURE 16.7 Continued.

3. The student must work at or perform in the Annual MHS Invitational Tournament. In addition, he or she must serve as a chairperson for the tournament. (This will require the entire day.)
4. The student must perform his or her presentation at one special event during the year (club meeting, theatre production, school assembly, or any function other than a tournament).
5. Forensics members who are placed on probation, for any reason, are automatically disqualified from lettering. (See "Guidelines for Forensic Participation" for probation explanation.)
6. Any student receiving three detentions during the forensic season (December–May) will automatically be disqualified from lettering.
7. The student must meet with the forensics director at least once a week during the season to work on his or her presentation. This may be fulfilled by performing and receiving comments from a panel of teachers as selected by the forensics director.
8. The student must successfully complete a semester of forensics. (This may be waived by the forensics director if just cause can be shown by the student that he or she was unable to schedule the class.)
9. Any student missing the bus will not letter and could be removed from the team.

FORENSIC SCHEDULE

February 16, Washington
February 23, Middleburg
March 2, to be scheduled
March 16, MHS Invitational
March 23, to be scheduled
March 30, Jefferson (League)
April 13, (Regional)
May 4, (State)

GUIDELINES FOR FORENSIC PARTICIPATION

1. The student must attend all scheduled tournaments and remain there until released by the director. (Total of 5.)
2. Vandalism, use of intoxicants and illegal drugs, or other conduct unbecoming a MHS representative at a tournament shall not be tolerated.
3. No student shall leave a tournament without the consent of the forensics director.
4. Student must ride the transportation as supplied by the school to and from

(continued)

FIGURE 16.7   Continued.

each tournament unless the forensics director receives a note signed by the parent and approved by an administrator, or has personal contact with the student's parent. Approval will be granted only if student is riding with a parent.
5. All students shall conduct themselves in a courteous manner while attending or hosting tournaments. Students will adhere to all regulations as set down by the host school.
6. Students who fail to attend a tournament they have been registered for shall reimburse the school the cost of their entry fee. (Any member of an IDA or Duet will also pay his or her partner's fee.)

Following are the only exceptions:

a. Absence from a tournament due to a death in the family.
b. Absence from school due to illness.

To be excused, the student's parent must make personal or telephone contact with the forensics director before the scheduled tournament.

7. All students will have their presentations selected by January 1.
8. Students shall meet with the director at least once a week throughout the season (December–May). The time and length of the meetings will be determined by the director.
9. The season shall run from December to May.
10. Every member must work or perform in the Annual MHS Invitational Tournament.
11. Any student breaking rules 2, 3, or 5 shall be put on probation for the next tournament. Probation will consist of attending the next tournament but not performing, or removal from the team.
12. Students must report to the bus by the departure time or they will be left. Being left because of lateness will result in the student paying for this fee (see rule 6). Any student missing the bus will not letter and could be removed from the team.

MAKEUP ROOM
Radios and tape recorders are not allowed in the dressing rooms during rehearsal or performance.

The makeup counters should not be sat on. The school or the theatre department is not responsible for lost or damaged personal property left in the dressing rooms.

FIGURE 16.7   Continued.

OPIE AWARDS

The annual Opie Awards will be presented after the final production of the season. The awards honor those students who have displayed excellence in theatre during the current theatre season.

Nominations are made in each category by the director of theatre. Selections will be based on dedication, attendance, cooperation, talent, attitude, and leadership.

Nominations will be made in eight different categories. However, if no nominations are made in a certain category, no award will be presented for that category. The categories are Best Actor, Best Actress, Best Supporting Actor, Best Supporting Actress, Best Featured Actor, Best Featured Actress, Best Crew Member, and Best Newcomer.

A student may be nominated for more than one award during the same season.

After nominations are closed, a secret panel of faculty members (selected by the director of theatre) who have seen each production will vote on the nominees.

List of Past Winners:

OUTSTANDING SENIOR

Each year a senior is selected as the Outstanding Speech and Theatre Student. The student is selected by the director of theatre and forensics. Selection will be based on participation (the student must take part in the theatre productions, cast, or crews, and be a member of the forensics team), attitude, attendance, dedication to two programs, leadership, and a proven asset to the school. Announcements will be made during senior awards. The student will have his or her name placed on a plaque with those names of past years. If the director so chooses, a separate speech or a separate theatre award may be presented, or no award may be presented.

List of Past Winners:

PATRONS

In September–October of each year, patrons will be solicited and listed in the different theatre programs for that season. This campaign of area businesses and district patrons will be conducted by either students of the cast and crews from the musical or by a parent promotional committee. The ads to be made available include Special Angel, Angel, Patron, and Sponsor (see Chapter 11).

PICTURES DURING A PERFORMANCE

Taking flash pictures or using tape recording equipment during a performance is not allowed.

(continued)

FIGURE 16.7 Continued.

STUDENT ATTENDANCE AT REHEARSALS, PEFORMANCES, & CONTESTS

Attendance at rehearsals, performances, and contests is required by all participants. Students missing more than two rehearsals will be removed from the show. Students will be excused from rehearsal to participate in other previously scheduled school activities by notifying the director in advance.

A student who is absent due to illness or death in the family will be excused. Parents must notify the director of such absence.

Only those students who have been cast in the show or have been assigned to a crew may attend rehearsals and cast parties. Parents, however, are welcome and encouraged to attend rehearsals.

THEATRE SCHEDULE

"Anything Goes"—November 12
"Cinderella"—January 15
"The Bad Seed"—March 24

TICKET POLICY

Tickets for each show will go on sale approximately one month before opening. Tickets to all shows will be sold on a reserved-seat basis. Tickets may be purchased from the director of theatre or from the high school office (555–6789 Ext. 123).

All tickets must be picked up and paid for at least two days before the performance.

No tickets will be held at the box office.

Mail orders will be accepted and filled by returned mail if time allows. Payment must accompany orders.

Any unsold tickets will be available at the box office the nights of the show.

Tickets may not be returned or exchanged.

FIGURE 16.7 Continued.

Index

About the Author

James R. Opelt graduated with a bachelor of arts in speech-drama and journalism education from Bowling Green State University, Bowling Green, Ohio, in 1976 and a master of arts in theatre and media arts from the University of Kansas in 1988. He taught at Clyde High School, Clyde, Ohio, from 1976 to 1981; Gardner Edgerton High School, Gardner, Kansas, from 1981 to 1987; and Olathe South High School, Olathe, Kansas, from 1987 to the time of this writing.

Mr. Opelt has completed workshops and graduate courses at Bowling Green State University, Findlay College, Ball State University, Emporia State University, and the University of Kansas, and has studied musical theatre at the Goodspeed Opera House in East Haddam, Connecticut. His productions have been presented at State Thespian Conferences. Mr. Opelt has conducted workshops at both State and International Thespian Conferences.

He was named the 1985 Outstanding Speech Teacher by his alma mater, Bowling Green State University. In 1986, Mr. Opelt was the first to be named Kansas Outstanding 4A Theatre Teacher and was presented his award by Kansas Governor John Carlin. After only one year at Olathe South, the faculty presented him with a 1988 Faculty Award for his advancement of educational theatre by writing this book. Mr. Opelt is owner and general manager of Costumes Unlimited of Olathe, Kansas, working with high schools throughout the country.